Author's Foreword

This book consists of a series of talks on Christian and religious life for our times, delivered in the hermitage at Béni Abbès to a group of brothers and sisters preparing to enter religion. The text is a revised transcript of the spoken word, as was also the case with the previous volume, *Concerning Religious Life* (Darton, Longman & Todd Ltd, 1975).

Although delivered in circumstances similar to the previous ones, these new talks adopt a different point of view and most of the topics discussed are as relevant to laymen as to religious. I hope they will prove useful to all who study them.

Cépie, March 4, 1975   René Voillaume

FOLLOW ME

The Call to the Religious Life Today

RENÉ VOILLAUME

FOLLOW ME

The Call to the Religious Life Today

Translated by Alan Neame

DARTON, LONGMAN AND TODD

5182

First Published in 1978
by Darton, Longman and Todd Ltd
89 Lillie Road, London SW6 1UD

© 1978 Darton, Longman and Todd Ltd
Originally published in France by
Les Editions du Cerf, under the title
Laissez-là Vos Filets

ISBN 0 232 51376 7

Printed in Great Britain by The Anchor Press Ltd
and bound by Wm. Brendon & Son Ltd
both of Tiptree, Essex.

Contents

Why Make a Retreat in the Desert?

The aim of the following reflections is to help you make the best possible response to the vocation now being offered you by the Lord. Some of you are going to pronounce your first vows in a few days' time, others in a few months, while some of you have of course done so already. The problem however is the same for all of you: to reach an ever deeper understanding of what Christ's call involves and to be in a position to respond to it worthily.

This retreat is at once solitary and communal. It is solitary because you have to enter that solitude where God alone has access to your deeper self, since the response that you are about to give and the act that you are about to make concern your relationship with God. This in turn will alter your attitude to yourself. And the retreat is also communal, since this act concerns and alters your relationship with the Church, with your brothers and with the Fraternity. Finally, it concerns your relationship with the world. Responding to the vocation to which the Lord summons you is not therefore something done in a moment once and for all, but something which should keep on transforming your life. This is what we shall be studying together. But right at the outset of this retreat, I want you to grasp what this call should mean for you.

A real retreat modifies our relationship with God, for even if we envisage the retreat in terms of the mission to which we have been called, this latter too has its roots in an encounter with the Lord. Furthermore, you have only to read your Bible over to see that all those men and women called by God to perform a mission were also summoned to deeper intimacy with him – to a very personal, heart-to-heart dialogue with the Lord who commissioned them. I need not cite examples: you are well aware of this, having studied those sections of the

Scriptures concerned with Abraham, Moses, the Prophets and, of these, the gigantic figures: Jeremiah, Isaiah and Elijah.

As the time for the coming of the Messiah draws nearer, God opens his fatherly heart with increasing intimacy through his messengers. With the calling of Mary, the mother of Jesus, that summons takes the form of almost complete possession by the Spirit of God. While Jesus, last and supreme messenger of the Father, his human mind and heart intent from the age of twelve on fulfilling his Father's will, feels the need to meet him in the lonely intimacy of the wilderness. In the wilderness he fasts, confronted on the one hand by what his Father's design requires of him and, finding these requirements more and more unqualified and absolute: confronted on the other hand by the physical events by means of which this design is to be effected during those few years of earthly life still lying ahead of him. John the Baptist, too, was prompted to go into the wilderness to prepare for his mission as Christ's Forerunner. Paul, touched by Christ on the road to Damascus, was also prompted to withdraw into the solitudes of Arabia.

And you will have to do the same. For it is not a matter for you of merely joining a brotherly community, or adopting a certain life-style, or devoting yourselves to activities of a practical sort, be they as evangelical and apostolic as they may, but of grasping the fact that these human promises must be the outward sign, the upsurge as it were of a much more far-reaching change affecting the depths of your very being.

We are talking in fact of a confrontation with God. Since you are preparing to make a promise to God (which is a serious step to take) or preparing to renew promises made already, you will have to confront God himself in the manifestation of his will that you should collaborate with him in his work of salvation. This effort on your part is all the more essential, given that we all too quickly forget what God requires of us and that we shall never stop discovering that our vocation constantly has new practical demands to impose on us.

And again, we have to pursue this search together, since we are called to live together and since our response to Christ's summons entails far-reaching changes not only in our relationship with God but also in our relationships with one another, in the deepest reaches of our being. Nothing indeed can escape the influence of the Lord's call in our relationships with the Church and with the Fraternity it is fitting therefore that this examination of, that this confrontation with, your vocation should take place here, in this chapel permeated with the meditations and prayers of Brother Charles of Jesus – the man through whom the Lord has seen fit to reveal the grace of our vocation to us.

This encounter with the personal design which God has conceived for each of you individually should transfigure your lives. But this cannot occur unless from this encounter you carry away new lights about the life you will have to lead: convictions imprinted on your memory to fortify your freedom with a view to giving yourselves to God – a process never to be completed until the end of your existence.

My aim is to help you discover what kind of demands your mission is likely to make on you. For, as regards the intimate encounter with the Lord, no word of mine or of anyone else can give you the right dispositions for this: the Holy Spirit alone can lead you to that, and then only depending on your desire, your humility and your love.

Meditate first of all on the kind of faith that Jesus demands of his disciples, for this is the absolutely essential pre-requisite of all perseverance in a life given to God. In the *Jerusalem Bible* there are two notes which sum up everything that I could say on this topic. I should like you to read them carefully. They will help you keep company with Paul and John, those two great witnesses to Christ, so possessed by him that their lives were entirely transformed as a result. Try by studying St Paul's epistles to discover the strength of his faith in Christ, of his boundless love for him, and how he discharged his vocation as it urged him forward day by day. In the writings of the Apostle John, as from a perennial spring, you will keep discovering what light the discovery of the mystery of the Word of God can generate in the human heart, when the Word is loved as brother, friend and God.

What is most important of all during these days of retreat is what God will teach you in the depths of the heart, and the convictions which his light will reveal to you. The more I meditate on the prayer to the Holy Spirit which we shall now recite, the richer in meaning I find it. How profoundly it expresses our need for divine life. Brother Charles wished his brothers to recite it every day. Give yourselves time to meditate on its verses.

Come, Holy Ghost, our souls inspire,
    And lighten with celestial fire;
Thou the anointing Spirit art,
Who dost thy sevenfold gifts impart:

2 Thy blessed unction from above
Is comfort, life and fire of love;
Enable with perpetual light
The dullness of our blinded sight:

3 Anoint and cheer our soiled face
With the abundance of thy grace:
Keep far our foes, give peace at home;
Where thou art guide no ill can come.

4 Teach us to know the Father, Son
And thee, of Both, to be but One;
That through the ages all along
This may be our endless song,
    Praise to thy eternal merit,
        Father, Son, and Holy Spirit. Amen.

II

Vocation: an Overwhelming Encounter with God

Here you are at Béni-Abbès in Brother Charles's hermitage after your months spent in the novitiate or your years spent in religion. In surroundings like these it may perhaps seem to you that everything becomes easy and free of problems. Some of you may even wonder whether this sort of interlude in your lives as Little Brothers may not be a little premature, hence out of place, while others again may be tempted to think of this desert setting as somewhat artificial. These varying points of view should lead us to serious self-questioning on the subject: for you are not here merely to imbibe ideas or attitudes of mind but, above all, to make a responsible decision as to what you are going to do with your lives. You all have lives to be led and you ought to be clear as to how you will lead them. It is not very easy to be a religious in modern times. Nor, on the other hand, has it ever been so challenging or important to be one. We cannot fulfil our vocation unless we fulfil every aspect of it.

When Brother Charles became aware that God was calling him, he expressed his reactions in the following words, '*As soon as I believed that God existed, I understood that I had no other choice than to live for him alone.*' How dearly we should like to know what next took place in his soul! For discovering that God exists, understanding that God exists, has happened to millions of people. We may even say that there is no such thing as a Christian who does not have intuitive faith in God's existence. And we wonder what it can mean to live for God alone.

Living for God: this surely means living our human lives to the full, responding to all the demands it makes – social life, I mean, pressing in on us from all sides with demands of love, demands of justice, of jobs to be done, of useful activities? Yet, at that moment when Brother Charles discovers God in a peculiarly intense encounter – for it was indeed an exceptional

13

encounter – he turns away from men: he leaves everything, abandons all his plans, puts his affairs in order, renounces his fortune, bids a decisive farewell to his family; particularly his farewell to his cousin involved a heart-rending emotional wrench, convinced as he was at the time that he would never see her again. He leaves without leaving an address and elects to bury himself in a Trappist monastery. What can this mean?

When Saul was thrown to the ground on the road to Damascus by the glory of the Crucified Christ, his life was turned upside-down, so totally and irreversably that the result seemed out of all proportion to the event. Saul was persecuting the Christians, he was officially in charge of liquidating a sect which seemed a threat to the future of Judaism, and he set about his task with passionate zeal. He was known to everyone for his zeal when suddenly, for no apparent or explicable reason, everything looked different. He felt obliged to deny the basic orientation of his existence, and did so on the spot, in the most utter ignorance, blindness and agony. Struck blind, he was obliged to put himself under the orders of a man whom he did not even know.[2]

Faced with a radical choice like this, resulting from an encounter with God, what do we mean by the religious life, by a vocation as a Little Brother, by an evangelical life? How are people looking at your life from outside, be they unbelievers, Christians or even religious, to understand what your vocation means? Possibly they will say that you appeal to them because you are still young, because you live together apparently loving one another; or because you share the life of the poor and have something new to offer in witnessing to charity and simplicity; and this, they will add, is *evangelical*. But this is only the outside of your lives. There is something else, and you will feel this particularly here in the desert while living a different sort of life. You know that this is only for a little while, of course, for a month, for a week. Even so, you are not likely to forget that, like Father de Foucauld, like all other religious, one day you heard the call to leave all, a call entailing a reversal of values: to leave what is known as *the world*, to leave useful occupations behind you. Very often I get pained complaints from parents who cannot understand why this kind of life should be right for their son or daughter, who has had a good education and even holds a professional qualification as a nurse, a teacher, a doctor or engineer. Wouldn't a social, or even a political, commitment be infinitely more useful to humanity and to the improvement of society? Wouldn't such devotion to the good of mankind be better served by getting married? And this seems all the more obviously true since there are excellent examples whom we could name. Does leaving all make sense anymore? And hasn't what is known as *the world* changed out of recognition during the last hundred years?

And this is why we have to face up to ourselves. We are well aware that if we want to become and be a man, we shall have problems to consider over our individual relationships with other people. Today we are all aware that the individual personality is conditioned by the sum of relationships situating him in the physical world. The social sciences draw attention to the influence of these relationships on the development and stability of the personality; by the same token, someone lacking the opportunity or means of developing a normal network of relationships cannot achieve a fully developed personality. Now, the aggregate of an individual's relationships is necessarily affected by the summons to '*leave all*' and enter religion.

To lead the religious life properly thus gives rise to problems over relationships, and this is the angle from which I propose to treat religious life while you are here. By not doing so, we should run the risk of overlooking the facts of human existence. The relationships of which our lives are woven are diverse. First of all, there is our relationship with God the author of our lives, our Creator, Father and Saviour. And this is the aspect of the problem which I shall be dealing with today. So, first of all, is there such a thing as a relationship with God? Is such a relationship possible? Does it exist independently of our relationships with other creatures? Then too, there is a whole complex of relationships with ourselves, for we each have an intimate life of our own known by the time-honoured phrase 'an inner life'. We have our thoughts, our desires, our intentions, our aversions, our passions and our wishes. And by the interaction of the sum of these relationships with the outside world we become aware of ourselves as distinct and unique, and discover what sort of

people we are. And we realise that we have no choice but to be
what we are. Then again, there are our relationships with
other people, be they our brothers, our connexions, our friends
or people in general. And finally, there is our relationship with
the cosmos, with the entity we call the world and that other
entity which we call history. This latter nowadays seems more
and more to control, condition and polarise human activity,
without anyone's being quite sure whether man is its master
or its passive instrument.

I refer you again to Brother Charles's example. He abandoned all in a radical change of direction in his life. In this, he
behaved exactly like St Paul, St Augustine, St Francis of Assisi
and a great many other people who have experienced an encounter with God conveying an urgent summons to change
the course of their earthly lives and adopt the very antithesis of
what would have been their normal way of living. For it would
be wrong to say that every genuine encounter with God experienced by a man or woman must necessarily entail such a
radical change of life-style. The Gospel shows us that, after
meeting Christ and often on his advice, many of his friends
continued to lead their family- and working-lives as before.
And by *normal life* I mean what conforms to an individual's lot
as it would seem that God has foreseen it in putting him on
earth – to live in society, to work and to raise a family. All
peoples share this conception of human life, characterised by
the search for love and the quest for justice and social achievement. If you are here at Béni-Abbès, this is because something
has happened in your life, something resulting from a personal
encounter with God, an encounter involving profound, I might
even say essential, changes in your relationship with God and
in your social behaviour. And we ought also to consider
whether a call of this sort does not also involve responsibility
for a mission entrusted to us. Once you are active, in the
Fraternity, in a given environment, you will find it easier to
realise that your vocation involves a mission. That mission is
to share the lot of the poor, to work with them for their liberation and, more than all else, to show them Jesus Christ.

When we contemplate the working out of God's immense
design for mankind in the unfolding history of the Church – a
design extending over centuries and encompassing generation
on generation – we are tempted to lose sight of our personal

destiny, to forget about it, to minimise its importance, because we are told we are a composite unit, an innumerable throng, a people and its destiny: the People of God. In the Old Testament, God was doing his best to mould a people, sometimes even, it may seem to us, at the expense of individuals used by him as intermediaries or instruments of that destiny. Yet we know, despite appearances, that a man would not be a man if he had no personal destiny. What would be the point of liberating a people and what would that people's salvation mean, if this were not achieved in terms of a personal destiny for each of that people's members? When I encounter God, I know that God will not use me merely as an instrument. When God chose Abraham and Moses, when he chose the prophets, when Jesus chose his apostles one by one and when today he goes on choosing men to follow him, this is above all else because he loves them. By his very choosing them, he means them to be his friends more intimate than before. Let us be frank: a mission performed in God's name would have no meaning, were it not originally based on a personal encounter between the messenger and the Lord who commissions him. Being a country's ambassador is a job which can be discharged without its involving the core of one's private life. Similarly, a trade-union post or a mission in politics. But when it come to a mission as prophet of God, of being, to quote St Paul, 'an ambassador of Christ', when we are called to bear witness with our whole being that God is God and that Jesus is the Son of God, that kind of mission cannot be limited to externals and needs must involve the depths of our inner life. It must be so. The moment the performance of such a mission becomes external to ourselves, we fall into clericalism, into officialism – a deviation from which even the religious state is not exempt. We cannot dissociate the mission incumbent on us as religious to preach the Gospel from this new intimacy established between us and God; for this sets all in motion and the mission is its product. God does not use men as he might impersonal instruments. Quite the reverse. By loving choice, he associates certain people with him to accomplish the mission he has in mind. The choice and the call involve a dual motion, the effects of which on our lives we shall do well to assess: God simultaneously summons and separates, he leaves his apostle in the world and yet withdraws him from it. And the reason for this is simple enough: that the apostle has not only a mission to accomplish but must also be with Christ and dwell in intimacy with him.

So I put the question again: What does it mean '*to live for God alone*'? For if Brother Charles summed up his vocation as this, many other people have used very similar words. St Augustine for instance in a fine expression, though hard to translate precisely from the Latin, said that man was so made that his heart was always anxious and restless, all the while it did not find its rest in God. Man is made for God – in his basic essence and structure. This is what the ancient author of *Genesis* was trying to say when in his simple language he tells how God made man in his own image.[3] We are all aware, despite appearances and whatever the present or future results of biological research, that a gulf exists between man and other forms of life, the present tendency to subordinate everything to the biological hypothesis – that man is only a higher, social animal which has managed to master language notwithstanding.

To live for God alone? Would this perhaps be to devote ourselves to solitary activities, to prayer and contemplation, in a life led apart and distinct from the rest of mankind? Why not live for other people? Didn't Jesus himself insist that there were two commandments, equally important, neither to be taken separately, by which we should fulfil the whole Law?[4] The Lord also tells us that there is no greater love than to give up our lives for those we love. Called to the highest form of love, we should therefore be ready to sacrifice our lives – life, our most precious possession – for love of others. Many great-hearted people do this. What scores give their lives in ideological conflict, in struggling for justice! They give their lives. But to understand the full implications of Christ's saying, we have to put it back into his own mouth and grasp the fact that he was talking about himself. Jesus voluntarily gave up his life, his earthly, human life, in agony and death. How could anyone sacrifice a supreme and absolute good like life without believing in an even great good? Agreed, the life we sacrifice is precarious at best; whether a little sooner or a little later, it vanishes anyway! I cannot sacrifice my nature, my being, but I can sacrifice my life. Didn't Jesus also say, '*What will a man gain if he wins the whole world, yet ruins his own life?*'[5] Now, giving up our life is not ruining or losing ourselves, since the whole mystery of Christ is there to teach us the contrary – that through death we find life.

Each of us is called to make the discovery of God at the cost of discovering ourself. We have to conquer ourselves to become responsible persons. We come up against our limitations and discover that the need to turn outwards, to open ourselves to others, is vital to us. Some people suffer from not being able to manage this. They are frustrated. Nonetheless, there in the depths of our own personality we find God's mark, the seal of his image within us. We have an inexorable need for truth, even when we neither know of what this truth consists nor how we are to find it. We need truth, we need authenticity, reality. We cannot live without truth; we cannot accept falsehood, nor be content to live in illusion. We know that the latter will destroy us. Where then does this truth about our existence lie? For we need the supreme Truth, a truth affirming the reality of our existence, the authenticity of our being, affirming that we are not dreams, that we are not objects with no future.

We also need love, a fine all-demanding love. For we also yearn for beauty, for something in the same order of creation as ourselves. We cannot be content with being limited beings, we are thirsty for eternity. Admittedly, like many other people, we may allow ourselves to become absorbed in current tasks to the point when we forget our need for the absolute, for eternity – or atrophy it in the endless activity of seeking it. As a result of this, we find nothing, or settle for a temporary satisfaction before resuming our quest. We take refuge in a sort of scepticism about the world and about ourselves. But when an encounter with God occurs in the light and grace of faith, we discover on irrefutable evidence – not demonstrable but, even so, vitally and personally convincing – that in God alone can we find truth, beauty, love and eternal life. And that is what faith is. It is precisely an encounter with a living God; it is not the product of theoretical knowledge or of philosophic reflection. It is not a conclusion derived from our personal search. It is a living certitude, a luminous conviction, forced on us, without our being able to demonstrate it. We then dis-

cover that we are made for God, by discovering his image deep
within ourselves.

Does this discovery of the essential 'me' imply preoccupation with self, with my personal destiny, to the detriment of
my giving myself to others? Not at all. We are then capable of
realising perhaps that our own personal discovery, our encounter with God, is also the greatest good for each individual
on earth, at whatever stage of development he may be.

We also discover that we cannot have this encounter with God
except in Jesus Christ, in whom the Father reveals himself.
For, in our search, we need a Truth above all truths, a Life
that is eternal. And such a truth can only be a transcendent
one, that is to say, beyond all created things, and hence
beyond all human search or grasp. Yet such a truth can mean
nothing to us unless it becomes near and accessible, unless our
God becomes intimate with us, with our most intimate selves.
Such requirements seem irreconcilable. This has always been
the stumbling-block, the unresolved question in most of the
religions which have admitted the problem. Thus Islam, having reached an exalted notion of God's transcendence,
preaches his inaccessibility and so rejects any possibility of intimacy. A God divorced from the creation, remote from his
creatures in the sanctuary of his holiness, becomes inaccessible by very reason of our own impurity: we are sinners,
wretches, we are not holy! And this is when God reveals his
loving compassion and when, in the Creator God and Maker
of all things, we find a Father, since he has made us sons. And
a whole new range of relationships between us and God opens
up for us in Jesus Christ.

Reading the Gospel with the eye of faith and by the light of
the Holy Spirit, you will soon discover that the route pursued
by the apostles and all the Lord's disciples was precisely that
of this discovery. They arrived at an act of faith permitting
them to discover the presence of a God who was humbly near
them, eating and drinking with them, understanding their
weaknesses, patiently correcting them, feeling fatigue, sitting
on the coping of a well while they went off to fetch some food.
And of this God they were compelled to attest – not without
running into frightful obstacles – that he was the Lord, the

God of Abraham, of Moses, the Mighty God and Lord of all things. The reconciliation of these two opposites: such is the mystery of the Christian faith. But this reconciliation between transcendence and familiar intimacy with men was not achieved until Christ with his humanity had passed from his earthly state to transfiguration by divine glory. Words fall short of expressing this. The apparitions of the Risen Christ are pale manifestations of an infinitely higher reality beyond the disciples' scope to grasp, and by these manifestations Jesus seeks to prove his identity with the Crucified whose scars he bears. He is henceforth the Lord of Glory, and the apostles have to pass beyond the concept of Prophet, of Man of God, to that of Son of God, and from the concept of Messiah, King of Israel, King of Righteousness, to that of Lord of Universal History, Master of the World.

The experience of the Risen Christ lies at the core of the apostles' faith and brings it to full fruiting. And so it is for us – we men of little faith. For without this fulness of faith, our consecrated life lacks true direction and even our lives as Christians lack true meaning. Hence, the reason why I referred you at the outset to those notes in the *Jerusalem Bible* was that they contain a definition of faith which seems to me peculiarly accurate. It is indeed the case that faith is expressed by an attitude of trust in God as Truth. We can confidently put our trust in Christ because he is the truth. And once we have encountered this truth in Christ, which is indeed the very truth of God, our trust is such that we can abandon our lives to him, that is to say, let him direct us by means of our obedience to him. In this attitude of trust and self-abandonment, we stop relying on our own ideas and resources. How unlike the present trend which, in a world of secularisation and scientific development, encourages man to assert a total independence of thought and action in everything concerned with human affairs. Be that as it may, man still finds himself at a loss as to everything concerning his ultimate end, his reason for existing, what is called the life of the hereafter, and to any solution to the problem of the existence and knowledge of God. At the threshold of this domain science cannot but confess itself helpless, even when to conceal its impotence it claims that this domain does not in fact exist. In this area beyond the limitations of scientific investigation, we have to stop relying on our own ideas and subordinate them to those of Christ.

At which point we are bound to put this question: Why and how are we to stop relying on our own resources? Are we summoned to stop making any effort of will with a view to liberating our energies to transform ourselves and work for the improvement of the world, when the distinguishing characteristic of our times is man's growing awareness of his own responsibilities, leading him to mobilise and organise his efforts to make them all the more effective? No: man would never be summoned by God to renounce his human responsibilities. But, in the domain of our relationship with God and when it is a matter of acquiring holiness so that we may become perfect *as our heavenly Father is perfect,*[6] in accordance with the command given us by Jesus, then we cannot rely on our own resources; we have to put our trust in the Word and in the power of him who reveals what is invisible to us and makes himself known to us as the only Holy One. Faith disposes us to accept the Word of God unquestioningly, without reservation, with a childlike heart, for the Word to blossom and bear fruit in us in truth. We receive the Word of God in our intellect and the Word leads us to give ourselves up to the transforming power of him in whom we have set our faith. Then Jesus, the Lord of Glory, the Word by whom all things were made, becomes the Close Friend too, the Son of Man, the echo of whose words and deeds we ourselves can recapture, the beating of whose heart we can detect, who first loved us. Jesus so near is also exalted at the right hand of the Father, the first-fruit of the dead. Now we grasp what happened on the road to Damascus when Paul, confounded by the revelation of Christ's glory, encountered the Risen Lord. At that same moment, he encountered the man whom he was persecuting, the man called Jesus, the man who had sown dissention in Jerusalem, the man whose teaching in the synagogue he rejected! Simultaneously he encountered the man, a prophet whose influence he was fighting, and the Lord of Glory, his God! He was blinded, couldn't see a thing, didn't even know where he was! Everything he believed to be true had melted away! Paul's blindness was symptomatic of what was going on deep within him: he would have to open his eyes to a different truth.

Such is the foundation of our faith and our vocation resulting from an encounter with God. Whatever form your life in the Fraternity may take, whatever obstacles you encounter in your life, you can be sure that none of these things have any point unless you are aware of responding to a call heard one day in an encounter with your God, an encounter in which he gave you to understand that he was asking you *to live for him alone.*

A decision of this sort is not easy to make, nor is it easy to make up one's mind what sort of life should be its consequence. Once again: what is meant by *living for God alone?* As result of this encounter with Jesus in faith, what are we to do? Don't we have a choice? Can't we get married, lead a normal life, work unselfishly to help men liberate themselves from evil and injustice, learn to love all men with boundless charity, try and bring a more humane community to birth where we live? Can't we set ourselves the aim of producing children and bringing them up to be proper men and brave Christians? Why not? Awareness of the demands of Christianity on the lives of the laity is sometimes characterised today by the consecration of married and family life to God by actual vows in church. In the light of this, the religious life may sometimes seem a little out of date. There is therefore a tendency to define it as an evangelical life involving solemn promises within society. With this in mind, people claim a greater freedom of action in religion and, so that it may permeate society as leaven does the dough, tend to secularise it as much as they can. Is this really what religious life ought to be, a life primarily dedicated to the service of God?

What Charles de Foucauld discovered, what other holy founders discovered before him, led them to institute a kind of life sharply differentiated from that of the laity. What was this life to be? Should we be content with the canonical definition given by the Church – a definition which seems out of date on a number of counts? Should a religious abstain from returning to life in the world? The expression *leaving the world* used to denote the initial act of the religious. What does that same act imply today? What are we to understand by consecrating our lives primarily and exclusively to the things of the Kingdom of God, to use the words of Vatican II?

We have already mentioned the *evangelical life*. It is time we were agreed on what this means. What is the Gospel? Many people own this little book. Nowadays it is no longer peculiar to Christians: unbelievers, members of other religions draw inspiration from it. And some use it, depending on the way they interpret it, to criticise the way Christians behave. For such, the Gospel is first and foremost a call for justice, a call to fight for the poor, a call for universal love and peace. Very true – but is this in fact the Gospel's essential message? And even granted that every Christian is compelled by his faith to promote charity, righteousness and peace, you could hardly say that the originality of Christ's Gospel consists in that.

The majority of the parables recorded in the Gospel had already been quoted in other rabbinical writings and were known. You may even find in the wisdom of the East certain teachings closely resembling the Sermon on the Mount. Some people, having studied the Gospel as purely human wisdom, go on to study Hinduism or Buddhism. Why not? The book of the Gospel is accessible to everyone and, detached from the person of Christ, is compatible with any ideology you care to name. What becomes of Jesus then, and if he is mentioned, which Jesus are we talking of? And when he declares that he has come to bring men eternal life, what construction are we to put on that? Before talking at random about *evangelical life*, wouldn't it be sensible to give serious thought to what this means? May we not otherwise all too easily end up agreeing that some unbelievers lead a more evangelical life than certain Christians do? As long as a man is devoted to the poor, whether he fights for justice or is imbued with universal love, people will say he is leading an evangelical life.

Now, Jesus says that the Gospel, the Good News, consists in the revelation of eternal life and in God's adoption of mankind as sons, and in this unparalleled fact that, by his Resurrection, he has conquered death. And whoever believes in him has life eternal. The love which the disciple is summoned to display for all men is one of the obligations of his new state as son of God. New depth is thus conferred on the love which we ought to have for one another. This behaviour, called evangelical, is thus a consequence: we must not divorce the consequence from what is the essential content of the Gospel message. To affirm that Jesus is Son of God and Saviour, and to believe in him: this is the Gospel. Yes, Jesus is Saviour, but how is he so? What sort of saving does he do? Jesus came to call men to repentance, so that he could give them eternal life.

And so we ask our question again: *What does it mean to live for God alone?* Is there a choice to be made between various ways of living? Are there different states of life? Do the distinctions between lay Christian life, religious life and other forms of consecrated life still exist? Aren't these distinctions out of date, even if still enshrined in canon law? Isn't it enough just to live as a Christian?

Arguing merely from the text of the Gospels, I do not see how we could reach any definite answer to this question. There will always be people who, having encountered God in this life, will see new demands to be met and feel impelled to turn their life-style upside down. Those who leave for the wilderness because convinced that God is calling them to abandon all so that they can live in intimacy with him by leading some kind of sacrificial life distinguished by total renunciation and entirely centred on intercessory prayer, do this in the name of the Gospel. And those who go off to fight shoulder to shoulder for human justice, to relieve the poor, to tend the sick, to evangelise the world, do this in the name of the Gospel. What then is human life? What form should it take?

We may try and define it in terms of the demands made by present-day societies and in terms of the ideologies governing them and themselves claiming precisely to define human life, its rights and its requirements. Today mankind finds itself living in societies which, owing to the complexity of their structure and to the ascendancy of the economic imperative, are increasingly restrictive. Is this the ideal way for man to live? For the fact is that if you want to produce a given effect on society, you have to accept some sort of ideology, that is to say, you have to have some idea of the society which you hope to construct. And the current ideal to which the system is intended to conform manifests itself in an increasingly scientific and technological idiom. Is this really the right direction for our living-patterns to be taking?

I am afraid I cannot prove what I am going to say by rational argument. I can only bid you consider the confused aspirations rising from the heart of man thus conditioned. But,

we have Jesus, the Son of Man, as he lived and as he speaks to the hearts of certain men; and finally we have the Church, of which we shall have more to say.

Jesus lived in a certain way. He was a man. But how did he lead his human life? Of those who met him and followed him, there were some who were so attracted to him that they wanted to live like him. Now, of course, every faithful Christian is like another Christ, he is a member of Christ and Christ lives in him. And this is true, whatever the state, profession, social position, in a word the life-style of that Christian. Yet the history of the Church shows us – and the call to the religious life which you yourselves have heard confirms this – that there are different ways of following Christ: by imitating or not imitating him in his state of life.

And the first thing perhaps that I shall discover is that Jesus was *chaste*. Can I imagine him as getting married, and having descendants and human offspring? I don't think I can even conceive of such a thing. Not because marriage is impure! This aspect of Christ's behaviour has a deep significance. Jesus was the most perfect, the most complete man that ever could be. In himself, Jesus prefigured the state in which men are called to become perfect and complete. For me, Christ's chastity means that there is something beyond human fertility, something beyond the love expressed in marriage, something beyond the life of the senses. Or should we feel bound to say that Jesus was not a complete man? But this is inconceivable. Now, if this state had significance in Christ's life, would it not be appropriate for him to call men to live like him in this respect? Did Christ intend to keep his chastity present among men by, as it were, prolonging that form of existence among them that was his? No one could answer such a question, had the Holy Spirit not already suggested an answer by prompting men and women to embrace that state of life and by inspiring the Church to approve their decision. For at first sight what possible purpose could this celibacy have? We know about the emotional problems to which the celibate life very frequently gives rise – especially since marriage is held in high esteem and it is easy to demonstrate the various advantages of companionship between husband and wife, even without mentioning that the married state enjoys the dignity of a sacrament.

I shall also discover that Jesus was *poor*. But what does this poverty consist of? We cannot define it merely by reference to preconceived notions about poverty as a sociological concept, or as mere non-possession of material goods. If we try to look as Christ as he was, we discover that his way of being poor transcended the merely human. He said so himself on several occasions and his behaviour demonstrated this at every turn. Christ actually uttered curses against wealth. Given the nature of man and his situation in the world, Christ sees in wealth the roots of materialism, of selfishness and an instinct to possess, asserting itself at the expense of others' good and interests. This is more than clear. But there is more than this to the poverty of Christ. For it asserts itself as a summons to what lies beyond the necessities of life, in so far as a certain degree of wealth, the ownership of certain goods and chattels, constitutes an environment necessary for human survival. But there is something beyond these needs, however essential these may be. And you only need to read the Gospel carefully and objectively to see that Christ's poverty makes the ownership of earthly goods a matter of merely relative importance. These goods are not what constitute the essential thing in human life, necessary though some of these goods are. And Christ expressed himself on the subject in terms that seem alarmingly forceful and certainly disconcerting, '*Look at the birds in the sky. They do not sow or reap or gather into barns; yet your heavenly Father feeds them! . . . And why worry about clothing? Think of the lilies growing in the fields; they never have to work or spin; yet I assure you that not even Solomon in all his regalia was robed like one of these*'.[7] This can't be put into practice for a start. And secondly, it is completely outrageous! Surely this is condemning working for a living? We have to understand what Jesus means by it. '*Fool, this very night the demand will be made for your soul; and this hoard of yours, whose will it be then?*'[8]

Clearly Christ was aware of something beyond life as we know it. His poverty shows that he regarded all earthly comfort as merely a relative good. This kind of vision of the world is radically at odds with the modern notion. We should not therefore look in the Gospel merely for an urgent invitation to give all men their fair share of worldly goods. There is more to it than that. And once again the question has to be asked: are some people called to share Christ's state of poverty and the state of mind arising from this, and to adopt a similar stance towards earthly affairs as that embodied in Christ's conception of them?

Lastly, Jesus was *obedient* to his Father, obedient to the last fibre of his being, for the Word became flesh with a view to accomplishing God's design. The reason for Christ's existence as man was to obey this design in all freedom. And this was what the Child was to discover on attaining the age of reason, when he became aware – humanly speaking, I mean, since the mystery is far beyond our powers of comprehension – that he was the Son of God. This awareness took place in terms appropriate to a thirteen-year-old boy, prompting him to say that he had to be busy with his Father's affairs.[9] His Father's design was not something he could avoid, he freely accepted it in full knowledge, out of love, although the acceptance was always very painful, since the design, involving suffering and death, ran counter to the most spontaneous aspirations of his human nature. The way for him lay past the cross. Jesus was truly and exclusively devoted to his Father's affairs. He had nothing else to offer mankind, he had nothing else to preach or to reveal, except the Father's loving plan of salvation, in other words, the gift of eternal life. He had nothing else to tell us, for after as before his coming on earth, men in so far as they are responsible for what happens on earth have nothing to expect directly from the Son of God. Jesus was not to teach us anything in the field of economic, social or political relations, of which the earthly commonwealth is composed. What was changed, or what ought to be changed, was the human heart: this is where the extension of the Kingdom of God takes place.

And so I come back to the question which we were asking before: Are some people called, not only to a total sharing of Christ's exterior way of life whether at Nazareth or in his evangelistic activities, but actually to living as he lived his personal interior life? Many prophets before him had pursued the same kind of activities, devoting themselves to spreading the word of God. An even greater number of righteous men have lived their lives in the same sort of exterior conditions as Jesus lived in his in Nazareth. What we are talking about is a much more intimate and personal conformity, not of imitating

Christ's exterior or social life, but of imitating his way of being a human being. We are talking about being called to continue Christ's mission by so sharing in it as to be chaste like him, with him and for the same reasons as his, in so far as it is possible for us to grasp what those reasons were, to grasp the meaning of the chastity of Christ, the Word of God made man. We are talking about being called to espouse the poverty of Christ, leading us to assign a merely relative value to human things. By this, I do not mean that we should undervalue human suffering, nor the love that we should bear for people, given the limitless demands that Christ's love for them made on him, but that we should share the Lord's own vision of human life. For this will enable us to grasp the fact that if people attach an absolute value to earthly things, whether because of the need they feel of acquiring them or because of actually possessing them, whether it be in the fierceness of their struggle to develop or to share this wealth, or in the egoism encouraged by wealth, these people lose any sense of Christ's poverty. They are not free. True freedom as regards things and the world can only exist in a man's heart when the life eternal takes first place. We are invited to share Christ's own vision of the creation. We share his vision of history, his vision of the consummation of all things by the glorification of human nature in God.

And we also share Christ's obedience, by being called to subordinate our whole lives to the requirements of a mission, which we agree to serve by becoming entirely dependent on that mission, in the sense of no longer exercising any choice over our own activities; our lives are then led in total obedience to the Father's design, in and with Jesus. A mission of this sort, being the prolongation in our own lives of Christ's life in his Church, cannot therefore be effective unless within that Church.

People may therefore be called by the Spirit totally to share not only the life of the Son of God, but also his way of being a man: his way of sharing in the human round, and his attitude to the affairs and history of the world. This is to be a prophet like Jesus and a witness to Jesus. This is not merely to be a witness to a certain kind of charity or brotherly love, but to a charity commensurate to a new dimension of human nature revealed in Jesus Christ. Being Christ's witness does not therefore consist in devoting ourselves to this or that external activity, however evangelical it may be: it means revealing Christ by letting him live in us, by letting him transform us into his image, however clumsy and imperfect the result. For a poor religious of good-will, who has faith in his call and who tries to let Christ live in him and in him continue practising his chastity, his poverty and his obedience, is indeed a genuine religious, despite his faults and failings, very obvious as these may be, provided that his intention is right, that he knows for sure that he has been called and does his best to respond to that call.

At the root of this type of life then, there is something telling us deep down in our hearts that Jesus has indeed called up to live like this. No one can demonstrate this for us. Nor can anyone control the intimate aptitudes that this call demands: that is a secret between God and the individual. This type of life, unique in that it participates in Christ's unique type of life, may however take a variety of forms, organisationally speaking, as for instance that of the Fraternity. And isn't it because you have encountered the Lord deep within you and he has turned your lives upside down by showing you that you were to leave all for his sake, that you have decided to come here? Yes, he has indeed invited you to leave all. This is the indispensable condition for joining Christ, even though, subsequently, you will recover things to which you used to be attached but from which, henceforth, you will be free. For Jesus was totally free as regards things. Some people accused him of drinking wine with sinners or of going to parties given in his honour by the rich. Jesus accepted Mary Magdalen's perfume. He was well above all that! Nor did he take a pessimistic view of any creature or of any of the things of this world. This notwithstanding, he was first, foremost and completely absorbed in his Father's affairs. How different it is with us! We cannot attain that sort of freedom without great effort and many self-imposed renunciations! We shall say more about this when discussing our relationship with ourselves, and then we shall see what far-reaching effects Christ's call can have on our most intimate personal life, at those depths which God alone can penetrate. Again I say: religious life does not merely mean committing ourselves to a kind of life only involving our external activities.

Let us take an example. If I want to be a priest because I feel drawn to the ministry and want to proclaim Jesus to men, it will be relatively easy for me to devote myself to the appropriate activities. If I go no further, however, I shall indeed have discharged a function, but my life will not be all that deeply changed – not even if I discharge my ministry in all conscientiousness and fidelity. Equally, I can be a competent teacher of theology, yet not live on intimate terms with Christ. Similarly, I can become a conscientious religious, faithfully observing the external requirements to which the religious life commits me, without even then making a personal commitment to Christ. For, unfortunately, an outward form of life can be distinct from an intimate, total self-giving to God. And, as regards ourselves in the Fraternity, our way of imitating the life of Nazareth can also be dissociated from the total giving of ourselves to God.

But now it is time to conclude. Faced with the various possibilities which life offers, and depending on the attitude which I have to the Church, as it exists, and to the world, as it exists, I realise that I have decisions to make and that various kinds of life are available to me. If I feel myself called to embrace that form of life of Christ's which seems to require me to withdraw from human affairs, I then begin to wonder how my life can still be useful to mankind. What is the truth about a life like this? Does it correspond to something real? I also wonder what value that life known as contemplative can have. To cut myself off in the desert, to bury myself in silence, to stay all by myself, immobile, inactive, to devote myself to the purely interior activities of communing with God in the hope and desire of acquiring light divine – how can I help thinking that a life of this sort is artificial?

Now, this is exactly how you will be living during this retreat. And of life in the novitiate, it has also been said that this is artificial, on the grounds that it is self-contained and insufficiently related to ordinary human life. But may it not rather be said that such types of life are concerned with a different aspect of life, just as real as, if not more real than, human life with its usual preoccupations? If I live like Christ, wouldn't it be logical to conclude that my life will be useful to

mankind in the same way as Christ's was? Make no doubt of
it: when you leave our desert hermitage, you will be joining
various fraternities where you will find a very different environment! How will you react? Isn't it a good thing now to
ask ourselves those questions which will spring to your mind
then? How are you to keep your inner eye fixed on the invisible realities of God's world? How are you to change yourselves
so as to be like Christ, and Christ's, in your relationships with
people in the world and in the tasks which they will ask of
you? For you will have to stay on constantly familiar terms
with God, for your lives to be transformed by him, for your vision of the world to correspond with Christ's and not with
men's; for your sense of history to be a Christian and not a
political one; and finally for you to retain a very pure sense of
your evangelistic mission and not confuse it with any other
attempts to make yourself useful to mankind.

Your vocation, you ought to know, can be a source of illusion; Nazareth can be the source of illusion; the contemplative
vocation, as also the vocation to political action or to
evangelism, can be sources of illusion. For the mere fact of full
participation in the life of a human group can never constitute
an absolute. The temptation will always be there to think that
sharing the conditions of the poor is the yardstick of your life.
Now, there is a concept of life and human activity, there is a
prevailing idea, there is, in brief, a concept of life which we
cannot share without denying the values of the Kingdom of
God, and Christ's design. What, we may ask, would Jesus
have thought and what would he have done if he were in our
shoes? An idle question, you will say, since no one can know
the answer! Even so, Brother Charles made this his rule of life:
to ask himself what Jesus would have done, if He were in his
place. A Christian living in the world will not ask the question
in the same terms as a religious will, since the tasks of the one
and the other are fundamentally different. Admittedly, the
religious is a Christian, but he has a special mission which
cannot be performed with the same freedom of action. For he
has to adopt the way in which Jesus, disregarding human considerations, lived his mission as Son of God. Not all Christians
are called to lead their lives like this: they have to perform
their earthly jobs, they have to rear their families and concern
themselves with temporal affairs, they have to work and

struggle to construct a more humane and just society. But the religious, by contrast, is called to be with Jesus, to be the prophet of the Gospel tirelessly proclaiming the requirements of divine justice; he has to debate with the world in the name of Christ's Gospel and sometimes to oppose the world as Jesus opposed it. Our's have to be Christ's reactions, as the Gospel records them for us. As a religious, I have to think of myself as sent by Christ to witness to his Gospel and it is my bounden duty to try to behave as Jesus himself behaved. Commissioned by him, I am his representative, I am an extention of him in his prophetic mission: which mission is an essential aspect of the Church, entrusted by her to those whom she summons to be her full-time, life-long evangelists and prophets.

We shall come back to all this again; meanwhile I was anxious to insist at the outset on something which has to be the basis of every religious vocation. I mean: an overwhelming encounter with God, in the sense that this encounter completely overturns life's scale of values. This encounter takes place in Jesus Christ and in faith, and it is not enough for it to have occurred at one given moment in time. We have to go on drawing new results from it and acting in such a way that our behaviour is influenced, transformed and, once again, turned upside down in the fullest sense of the expression: for no one could spontaneously live as Jesus Christ once lived. I say 'spontaneously', even though this type of vocation corresponds to the deepest aspirations of our being as we discover them at the exact moment of the encounter. By this we know that such an encounter has really and truly taken place. This is when, with inner certainty, we are sure that God is really asking us to make him a total gift of our lives.

III

In the Luminous Assurance of Faith in|Christ

To talk about our relationship with God is to touch on the deepest, most essential and most personal aspect of our lives. It also means tackling a subject productive of every sort of effect in every sphere of life. Hence the difficulty of talking about it. Let me say now that I shall be talking in terms of situations not yet applicable to you here as novices at Béni Abbès, but with which our fraternities at large are often confronted and of which you ought to be forewarned.

It is obvious that our relationship with God, I mean above all that person-to-person relationship of creature to Creator, of son to Father, can only be initiated, be thought out or be experienced, in faith. Only at the level of faith and by the light of faith, is it any use our trying to develop this relationship.

What then is faith? Since you are now living by it, you perhaps do not need me to define it for you, and you probably do not feel the need to question yourselves about it. You will soon, however, be obliged to live among men, among Christians, for whom the question does arise, and even to meet priests and religious who are subject to self-questioning about this. And one of these days you yourselves will find that you are no longer so certain what it is! It is not impossible that some of you may be forced to ask this question in environments alien or even hostile to religion. Faith, then, is the confident acceptance in boundless self-abandonment of the Word of God as he reveals himself. Faith is essentially and primarily concerned with knowledge of God, of his designs, particularly of those to do with the destiny of man. This handing-over of the mind to God is in fact an abandoning of it to the mind of Christ through his word; it is a sharing in Christ's knowledge of his Father and of his Father's wishes. Yes, up to a certain point we can say that faith involves participation in

Christ's own experience of the Father. How could this sort of faith be merely a vague feeling? How can it not be of the order of real knowledge – as though our intellects were possessed by the reality of the divine world? *'Have I been with you all this time, Philip, and you still do not know me? To have seen me is to have seen the Father.'*[10] Even so, it is not very easy to grasp a discovery like this! *'To have seen me is to have seen the Father.'* What does Christ mean? Many men have seen him, met him, listened to him and not believed in him, and therefore have not *'known the Father'*. Besides, we are perfectly aware that Jesus was not the first person to reveal the Father to us. Before him, there were the prophets, not to mention all the events revealing God's intervention in the directing of human history, in the gathering, liberating and training of his people Israel. In all this, God was revealing himself to men. Yet there is a fundamental difference between what we can know about God before Jesus Christ and after Christ, the Incarnate Word of God. Yes, God did indeed speak through historical events by signs, by deeds, by prophets inspired by his Spirit and interpreting his designs to men. But in Jesus, God revealed himself in those most intimate aspects of his life: the enduring, living relationships of fatherhood and love which no created being had been able to discover on his own and the existence of which could not even be suspected.

Such is the mystery, veiled, yet shining through the face and life of a man subject to the limitations of the earthly condition. This man, Jesus, expressed himself in the Aramaic language of his day, in terms of a contemporary Jewish culture. In spite of this, his witness has the force identical with that of eternal truth, transcending the limitations of every language, of every culture, of every human means of expression, since this was the very Word of God, bearing within itself the seal of its own truth for anyone ready to receive it without questioning, with a humble, attentive heart, and prepared to accept the consequences that such a Word is bound to have in our lives. Without dispositions like these, we should not be able to know Jesus as he is and to understand him. In his person, we are given understanding. Yes, I mean this: understanding of the mystery of God – an understanding absolutely impossible to convey by the normal means of human knowledge, but nonetheless a real understanding of God. If we accept the Word in simplicity of heart, it will be given us to know God – an indistinct knowledge perhaps, but nonetheless true and limitlessly perfectable, for it can always be deepened in the enlightening and loving relationship established between the individual and the Father.

This knowledge of the intimate life of the Trinity can be ours by faith, be our attainments in the academic field as great or little as they may! Make no doubt of it: rational enquiry is both lawful and needful – as conducted through the ages, but most particularly in our own day. Historians, textual critics, philosophers study the Scriptures to grasp their meaning more exactly; and progress can always be made in this. And indeed we should never stop trying to improve our own understanding of the sacred text, by using all those means normally available to us in other fields of human enquiry. But over and above this sort of knowledge, and at a different level, another kind of understanding is given us by the Spirit of Truth, promised to us by the Lord and sometimes revealed to us without our always realising what has happened. There is a great deal of talk about the Holy Spirit today. But talk of this sort should always be governed by the discretion and respect appropriate to the depth of this mystery – for the Spirit of Truth does not reveal himself to all comers in all situations. Fulfilling Christ's promise, this Spirit, being his, will make us understand what Jesus himself has told us.[11]

Too often we forget that in this deepening of our knowledge by faith, we are all involved in a co-operative effort. How can we hope to make progress on our own when our experience is so limited, and so subject to illusion or to error? Our knowledge of Jesus, of his mystery, of his Father revealed to us by him, must needs be strengthened, nourished, widened, deepened by the insights and universal experience in time and space of the Church, herself continually synthesising and memorising every gainful experience, every atom of contemplated truth communicated by her members incessantly ever since men, once having received the gift of faith, began reflecting on the person of Jesus Christ, on his teaching and on the content of his Gospel message.

It is important to get this into our heads, for we are led by faith into the fulness of a living reality, bearing us up, overflowing in all directions: the reality of the Body of Christ, the members of which we are..

Faith is strong, it is not weak; faith is firm, it is not shaky; being the reflection of the truth of the Word of God, even if faith is not plain, this is only due to the difficulties which we put in the way. Owing to our blind-spots, our refusals, our limitations, we run the risk of losing it, and must constantly seek means of strengthening it, of making it grow and, above all, of making it live. For faith concerns our whole existence. On it depends our future and the future of mankind; hence faith cannot but influence every aspect of our behaviour.

The intimate knowledge of God which is given us in faith has to culminate in the meeting with a person; just as the apostles had gradually to learn to know Jesus until the day when they were led by the Spirit to confess that not only was he a prophet but the only Son of the Father. For three of them, this faith was fortified by the vision of their Master glorified on Tabor, and later it was fortified for all of them by his exaltation at the Resurrection. Each of us is led by a similar path, often long and strewn with ordeals. And such a road is always beset by darkness, failures and fresh starts. Even so, as soon as faith exists, it is strong, it is true, it is real. We can sustain our lives on it, we can die for it. To reduce faith to a vague, indefinite feeling is in some degree to refuse it, to question what it is; it is a lack of readiness to abandon oneself to it, to abandon onself to it by renouncing one's own ideas and one's own resources.

Now, of course it is not easy to get to know someone! After all this long time spent living together as brothers, can you be sure that you really know one another? And yet, you know that your brother is beside you, certainly living and real. He exists, but you have only a hazy awareness of him. By his gestures, looks, words and reactions, you try gradually to find out what is going on inside him, in his heart, but you are never quite certain! On the other hand, you do know that he is really there and that he is as real as you are yourself.

And so it is with Jesus. In him, God is just as real for us as the brother or the sister sitting beside us. In a sense he is even more real. As we shall be saying in a moment – for we cannot say everything at once – if we concentrate too much on analysing, however scientifically we do it, the human vehicles adopted by the Word of God in approaching us, languages, for instance, cultures or historical events, we run the risk of stifling the Word. We must never forget that there is something beyond language, something beyond modes of expression, and beyond imagery. You know that some people now go so far as to question the value of the Nicene Creed, our *Credo*, on the ground that its various articles no longer convey any meaning to contemporary man. We run the risk of clinging to the expression, to the wording of the creeds, and so forgetting the realities that these expressions, these creeds merely denote. It would be a mistake to think that Christians living in the days when the Creed was drawn up saw no further than the expressions and the imagery of which they were making use. They knew what they were trying to say and by means of these simple statements of faith attained a whole deep, mysterious, invisible reality. Whereas we stop short at these surface-statements to argue about them. How should we go about expressing these same mysteries? I sometimes fear that people will give up trying to express anything at all, on the grounds that God cannot be known, cannot be understood and that therefore nothing can be said about him. Then, presumably, there will be nothing that we can do. How can man, immersed in the tangible universe, express his knowledge of the invisible God – the greatest gift indeed that God has given him – except by creeds? Are we going to find an alternative language to that of the Bible? There is, it is true, an understanding beyond the sense and beyond all expression, devoid of all ideas, imagery and forms, which the Spirit of God may communicate to our souls in a matter of seconds or even over an extended period. St John of the Cross was the exponent of this un-knowing, but in a very different sense from that given today to what is called negative knowledge. This latter sort of non-knowledge is not something beyond knowledge, but a negation of knowledge. The Christians who painted those wonderful frescoes adorning many medieval monasteries and chapels, representing heaven and hell, the devil and the angels in simple, graphic terms, were no simpletons! It would be insulting them to think that they imagined heaven or hell to be as they depicted them. Fra Angelico, with his luminous paintings of angels dancing in meadows sown with daisies, knew much more about heaven than we do! We can, of course, jettison all that in the name of cool and critical rationality. And indeed we may be inclined to do so, emphasising the limitations and inadequacies of all religious symbolism. But how do you replace such simple, genuine expressions, instinct with the poetry of a world beyond our own, once having decided that purity of faith demands that we reject all forms of representation? I am well aware that the development of our prayer-life towards true contemplation consists precisely in leaving all imagery behind. But it is not in our power nor is it right for us to repress the simple pictures and concepts we may form of the face of Christ and the mystery of the Life Divine. God does not repress them; only, he bestows such fulness of knowledge on us that everything else, all our human modes of knowing things, grow dim and fade away, since we then know in a way transcending those ways of knowing available to reason and the senses. For this is actually a living experience of God as he is. This is what contemplation means.

Hence I repeat, faith is in itself strong, it is solid even when it is barely rooted in us or when it finds it hard to express itself, even when we feel that we cannot share it with others. For it is not in our power to bestow faith on someone else, whereas we can teach him mathematics or history, given that he accepts us to be competent. We cannot demonstrate the truth of faith, it being simultaneously and mysteriously a gift and an act of our free-will. The effect of faith is to introduce us to a real but invisible world, the world of God. Every Christian, by the sole fact of having faith, is inducted into this knowledge of the Lord, which is then reflected in his life. Which life he must thereafter lead, if he means to be faithful, in serving that Light, in serving the final accomplishment of the coming Kingdom of God now revealed to him.

This is where, as I have already said, the divergence between lay and religious life occurs. And the difference between them must be maintained. If not, the religious life no longer means anything and you might as well return to the world and get married. Yes, the fundamental characteristic of, and essential reason for, the religious life is that you make yourself available for Christ to possess you completely, at every level of your life, mind, heart and actions, so that through you he may continue his evangelising task and prophetic mission, and in so doing reveal all the beings and truths of the invisible world. Even if religious life takes the form of a limited incardination in society, it postulates a more vigorous faith, to make us live in more absolute contact with this invisible reality, not merely so that we can reveal it to others, but primarily because Christ wishes us to belong so totally to him as to hand over our whole earthly destiny to him.

The living presence of Christ you should aim to make habitual in your lives. This is not easy. You are in retreat here to discover the best way of achieving this prolonged and permanent intimacy with the Lord – a relationship which I shall not attempt to describe since no one can do so. You are loved by him who has brought you into existence, you love him in return and behold, you are at the source of your life! Many things will be revealed to you from time to time, and this will seem the most important thing in the world to you. Time no longer exists when the Lord admits us to this degree of intimacy with him. Even so, we can forget these encounters, we can lose the habit; in a word, we can change, by drawing away from him.

The gift of faith is something freely given, but not given to everyone. Yet, if it is not in our own power to acquire it, once we have received it, the gift is unequivocally ours. We can let it evaporate. As the Apostle Paul says, we are carrying a treasure in a fragile vessel. We are vulnerable, we are fragile. It would be a disastrous mistake to imagine that faith and the Lord's summons have made you so invulnerable that henceforth you can go where you like, devote yourself to any activity you like and live any way you like, without the risk of losing it. The Lord's gift has been put into your hands, confided to your responsibility, to be guarded by your intellect and heart. The owner of what has been entrusted to you will call you to account one day. You cannot go on living as though you had never received it, and many aspects of your life will have to bear the mark of it.

The reality into which faith inducts you constitutes an entire world, with its own demands and with a gamut of certainties. Hence, he whose faith has been fortified by contemplative grace, who has been enlightened by the Spirit of Truth – and this you all have been in so far as you have become aware that your lives belong in a special and exclusive way to God – must be realistic about the invisible world of God. But maybe you have already forgotten it, for the memory of the Lord's visits is all too easily lost.

Yes, faith admits us into the reality of a world, the centre, light and soul of which is the Risen Christ. And that world is immense. By faith, that world is already apprehended as present; yet it is also awaited as the supreme future for us and for all men. It is the invisible world, the universe which science cannot reach, the existence of which it can calmly deny. The manifestations of the invisible universe in human history, whether in the history of the Chosen People or in the unfolding of Christ's earthly life, may indeed be analysed as simple historical events. This universe is completely undiscernable: this is why so many people do not believe in it, and also why our faith is so fragile. The invisible world is the world of the angels, of all spirits, those of the dead, those of the saints; it is the Kingdom of the Divine and Personal Trinity, of Jesus in his glorified human nature. And where this Kingdom of God emerges here-below is in the human heart. Only in the heart does the Kingdom emerge explicitly, in so far as faith attains that world. We can perceive its effects in so far as we are transformed by it. Of this invisible world, the Kingdom of Truth, of Life, or Love, we see no more than an indirect reflection in the behaviour of the saints, but that world itself, as it actually is, we cannot perceive here-below.

When someone close to us is dying and we are present at his death-bed, when we receive his final breath, we witness the extinction of his earthly existence. We observe that a life has come to an end; we cannot see the other life. Everything seems to be over. Only an earthly shell is left, the remains of what was once a man, a well-loved friend. Nothing indicates the existence of a world in which the man who has just died actually goes on living. Even so, for us to have the right attitude to our terrestrial world and to order our behaviour as human dignity requires, we must fix our minds on the visible and invisible reality as a whole. Our lives being framed, immersed, in the terrestrial world, the contemplative aspect of our lives reveals the invisible reality of the divine world. This is precisely what contemplation means – a word so commonly used that people have forgotten what it does mean. We are forced to admit that there are two universes: if not, what would faith be? Faith would be nothing.

It is a good thing to have these matters straight, if you are properly to understand what I am going to say next, since this is both a sensitive and very important problem, particularly in so far as it concerns the vocation of our own fraternities. I mean the problem of faith in the world, especially in our day. The problem is far from being a simple one, given that we are living in a world which I should call scientific and ideological. These two characteristics engender a rationalistic attitude of mind, which is itself fatal to faith. The present-day attitude of the world is entirely conditioned by a point of view in which faith no longer plays any part, where God no longer has anything to say. I mean the whole contemporary outlook as expressed in modern ideologies. And here, or course, I exclude the experience and aspirations of those people, above all of the poor, who have turned of their own accord to Christ. The great mystery of human existence with all the concommittant questions about human destiny and the meaning of the world — that reality embracing past, present and future, contemplated by Jesus and glimpsed by the saints — is not something easy to deal with in contemporary life.

Faced with the mystery of the meaning and purpose of the universe as revealed by the Son of God, men have reacted differently at different periods. There was, for instance, for many centuries, a tendency to underplay the reality of the world, to minimise the importance of human affairs, since these were seen as transitory. The world was a place of suffering; life had to be led in expectation of the world to come. Life in union with Christ was seen as the sole reality, dominating all others: hence the radical separation from the created world which used to characterise the religious and contemplative life, which could then unfold in ignorance of this world's business. It was right to be detached from a transitory world, the true objective being life eternal. Viewed like this, the world seemed of secondary importance, an attitude unopposed either by the science or by the philosophies of the day, since these too placed little emphasis on the material, terrestrial world. This notwithstanding, the effects of the Gospel were certainly to be seen in the lives of many great-hearted

Christians, labouring often heroically in the cause of charity and justice. People did not wait until the twentieth century before clear-headedly and intelligently devoting themselves and their lives to these aims, but they did this in a different perspective, as the needs of the age dictated and without their activities' coming into conflict with the political and economic systems then universally accepted. They worked within an accepted structure.

Today, the situation seems to have been reversed. It is extremely hard to maintain a balance between the two universes, that of faith and that of the terrestrial world. The future of the terrestrial world is the sole preoccupation of most people, and for the rest, for Christians too, it is, if not the sole then at least the primary preoccupation and the only one of immediate interest. As far as the other universe is concerned, people think it will be time enough to bother their heads about that once they have reached its threshold. Man only possesses this invisible world by faith, fragile at best − and what little knowledge he has and the importance he attaches to it are both easily extinguished. It is easy to live in ignorance of this other part, God's part, of the universe. The Christian thus finds himself uncomfortably placed since he is immersed in a cultural environment conspiring to empty his faith of any valid or communicable content. Generally speaking, religion is at a discount. And a large number of people do not even seem to possess the intellectual apparatus which permits them to grasp a reality other than that gauged by experience. The Christian himself is no longer quite sure how to evaluate the knowledge which comes to him by faith, as against that conferred by modern science. Hence the tendency to emphasise the effects of faith, its repercussions in life, without bothering too much about faith itself. And thus the Christian is tempted to define himself in terms of the demands made by a loving commitment to the cause of justice, of universal love, of respect for man and especially for the poor. All this is good and right as far as it goes but these ideals are likely to fade soon if cut off from roots firmly set in a vision of man such as Christ had and which Christ shares with those who abandon their minds to him in faith. All too often, doubt lodges in the Christian's heart as to the reality of that invisible universe where the communion of saints occurs, the world of God, of the Risen Christ and the angels, of the Kingdom of God, whose enemy is Satan. All this seems vague since it is no longer positively affirmed, even when it is not categorically denied. And hence we are faced with the question: whether the invisible universe of God has primacy over the world, or whether in our own times that primacy lies with the world and its struggles, though not necessarily to the exclusion of the other world from the believer's mind. You may say this problem is nothing new! Great geniuses of the past have had this global vision of history: St Augustine expressed it in his wonderful panorama of the '*Two Cities*'. We cannot accept his concept as our own, but he had perceived the drama of mankind which haunts the minds of many noble-hearted men today. Things are much simpler, if I may say so, for the materialist. For him, there is only one world. Hence the strength of those ideologies inspired by a materialistic interpretation of history, since there is always a certain strength to be derived from only having one simple idea. The Desert Fathers, from the opposite point of view, evinced the same potent dynamism, deriving from an absolute view of the universe. They fled from the world and lived in expectation of the supreme encounter with God in total austerity, rejecting all earthly satisfaction, and some indeed, all human considerations.

Now, the charism of Brother Charles of Jesus – and this was to be reflected in the mission of his fraternities – prompted him, without resistance on his part and with the spontaneity of love, to accept this duality of worlds and embody its effects in his way of life. Would it be presumptuous or unduly ambitious to say that our vocation should make us the witnesses, I might even say the visionaries, the seers of the invisible world while living in the world of men and at the same time being not merely sympathetic but available to men in their cares and day-to-day preoccupations as they struggle to liberate themselves? Can this be done? What is the value of such a mission? That is the question I have to ask.

We are obliged to face up to this situation since it is one of fundamental importance. And in so doing, we shall be able to identify the problems to which this vocation gives rise, the risks which it will entail for us and the means by which it can best be discharged.

I have, I know, offered you an over-simplified analysis of the situation. But this is a risk that has to be taken when trying to come to grips in a few moments with a universal and very complex situation. Even so, certain features are immediately apparent. When I say that one of the characteristics of present-day Christian life consists in a greater attention being paid to the political and social effects of the Gospel message, I mean this in a positive sense. The Christian message is regarded as the principle capable of generating the energy required for the task of liberating mankind, and this we cannot help but situate within the context of a particular interpretation of world history, over-simplified no doubt and quasi-marxist, in which society is seen as being inevitably made up of oppressors and oppressed. It is always dangerous to simplify facts to this extent, since ideological abstracts of this sort take no cognizance of life's fulness and variety. Even so, this is a situation which we have to accept. As things are, the people with whom we have to deal see the world in these terms. And Christians have to adapt themselves to these conditions while bringing the spiritual dynamism of the Gospel message with them.

And at this point we may well ask what is left of Christian identity, once the reality of the invisible world and expectation of the coming Kingdom of God, not to mention contemplation of the Tri-une Godhead, that is to say, the Living God, source of all love and author of all being – once this, I say, has been pushed into the background. And the question is indeed constantly being asked: What is the specific role of the Christian in the world? What is the specific role of the consecrated religious?

And in the solutions proposed to the question we can distinguish as it were two periods. To spread ourselves a little in thinking about this is not to digress from our main theme – quite the contrary; for we have to investigate the demands made by our vocation as thoroughly as we can. You will realise how necessary this is, once you leave this hermitage and its surrounding desert and plunge back into the world of everyday life. I was saying: there have been as it were two stages in this enquiry – stages of which you are all well aware and on which I shall therefore merely touch. In the first instance, people tried to define the Christian's role here-below in terms of politics. The Christian was to be different from other men even at the level of social organisation and the construction of the earthly city. People envisaged a return to a Christian society, and planned to build a Christian city: hence there would be a Christian polity. You can see for yourselves how this has turned out in the history of the so-called Christian nations of Europe. This concept is now out of fashion. A little while ago, at a conference of Catholic thinkers, the same question was put, but the conclusion reached was that there was no specifically Christian role to be played in temporal affairs. What distinguishes the Christian is his faith. But as far as temporal activities are concerned, Christians are just like any other people who behave as responsible members of society. Jesus never revealed anything with direct bearing on politics.

The Christian is nonetheless obliged to consider what effect his faithfulness to the Gospel is likely to have in terms of political action. It seems to me that a Christian's attitude in politics may be summed up as that of deep respect for the individual and for the rights of the individual. And the Christian, believing that man is made in the image of God, that the poorest of men, the most useless of men, bears the image of the Lord within him, will have an infinite respect for him, regardless of what his abilities, his qualities and his achievements may be. The saints, having drawn near the heart of God, have always shown this infinitely respectful attitude to the individual as he is. This is why they have shown such respect for the poorest, for the sick, for the rejected, for those who cannot make themselves heard and who exert no influence here on earth. Not for any political reason, nor with any intention of manipulating them, have Christians felt it their duty to respect the political aspirations of the poor and to defend their rights. When corpses begin to pile up in the streets or the countryside because men are fighting to impose some ideology or other, we are obliged to wonder whether man has not been reduced to the status of object or instrument. At the sight of these corpses, how can we avoid having doubts about what survives of these lives sacrificed for a political motive? Anyone who has seen the carnage of the battlefield will understand the force of the question. If this is where it all ends, what is the point of my respecting the individual? – since the individual is merely used by others to build a given type of society or to ensure the triumph of economic imperialism or of revolutionary ideology.

Almost everywhere movements are springing up in defence of the rights of the individual, human rights, to prevent man from being used as an instrument. But who is really in a position to assert that man is in fact a subject and not an object? That he is a subject, worthy of such infinite respect that no ideology, no earthly reason, should allow anyone to infringe his dignity and his basic freedoms? No materialistic ideology, even when asserting this dignity, can advance a concept of human nature to justify the assertion; whereas the Christian will always find that he has a role to fulfil in this field by asserting the absolute rights of the person and by playing down wealth, profit and power, which he can never accept as being the ultimate good of human society. In this, the Christian finds himself at one, thank God, with many other men who, though they do not share his faith, bear witness to an equal respect for man. Furthermore, when it comes to the task of transforming society for the better, many non-Christians are way ahead of Christians, the latter not being intelligent enough or brave enough to bring their behaviour into line with their faith. And this very decadence is the reason why some people define Christianity in terms of socio-political action. According to them, by taking up this position, you can be a Christian without having faith!

When Christianity is viewed like this, what then becomes of Jesus? Well, after all, the Gospel is a book, a book like many others. And it can be read as we read other books or collections of human wisdom. Many religions, Islam, Hinduism, all have such works. As a profound product of human wisdom, the Gospel casts its spell over many men today. And this is how it is regarded, independently of and unrelated to the revelation of God in the world.

Read the Gospel again, read it again in the light of your faith, in the light of the faith of St John the Apostle and of the other apostles, and you will see for yourselves how Jesus reveals himself in it. To broach the Gospel and understand what it is really saying, you must at least have faith in the God of Abraham, you must be able to take your place with Christ's disciples and listeners, who were similarly prepared for believing in him. If I begin reading Christ's teachings while uncritically professing a materialistic or marxist ideology entailing a certain view of the universe, the Gospel may indeed be of interest to me on some points, but I shall nonetheless interpret it in terms of my own concept of man and history, and reject everything alluding to God, to the existence of God and to the divinity of Christ, as myth induced by the religious notions current at its time of composition. This is the way many people read the Gospel to day. And we may well wonder whether many Christians are not equally satisfied to take this same reductionist view.[12]

Yes, the Gospel may certainly be read in dissociation from the person of Jesus, of the living, risen Jesus. And then the Gospel appears to be a liberation message, a message brought by someone who had courage enough to compromise himself and sealed the message he brought by dying for it. The Gospel read like this, Jesus was condemned to death for having challenged the religious establishment, for having opposed the doctors of the Law. He died a victim to an established religion and social order, which he had challenged by his calls for justice and respect for the poor. For the Gospel – and this is why it appeals to so many people – is based on a notion of man and life for which people are thirsty today, particularly the younger generation. Jesus as author of the Gospel is sought, people no longer fear him, he no longer inspires an awed respect. A new picture of Christ is gradually emerging and becoming accepted – with the remarkable result that Jesus is now more preached about outside the Churches than within them. Even business is now exploiting the Jesus-craze! But there is more to it than that. A new picture of the Lord is emerging: of an innocent man unjustly put to death, someone to be identified with every poor unfortunate sufferer. Here are a few significant examples. First of all there is the protracted run of *Godspell* in New York, London and Paris. Now, I doubt very much if the caste of young actors who have been staging and absorbing St Matthew's Gospel for months on end has come as a result to believe in Christ's divinity. Their lives have, I am sure, been influenced by their experience and from what I know of the Paris group it seems that they may shortly turn their attention to the wisdom of the Hindus. The Gospel will merely have been one stage in their pilgrimage.

This picture of Christ as prophet and master of wisdom is neither opposed nor offensive to any ideology and is indeed acceptable to most of them. The accentuation of this human wisdom, of this concept of man contained in the Gospel, may certainly give many Christians food for thought and make them realise that their own reading of the Gospel should lead them radically to reconsider their attitude to man and to society.

Then there is the film *Jesus Christ Superstar*. And here again we have the same sort of thing: there are moving moments, a certain heroic quality, but again we only have Jesus the man. And so it is in pop-music too. The figure of Christ emerges time after time as the personification and symbol of man oppressed; while Jesus himself is always represented as seeking further wisdom. This kind of Christ rouses no opposition. He is proclaimed outside the Church under this new guise, putting him within everyone's reach.

The diffusion of this particular image of Jesus possibly constitutes a greater obstacle to the genuine preaching of the Church than a refusal or denial of Christ. As man, Christ is accepted, he is loved, he is followed as a sage, and people do not even bother to deny his divinity: the question is passed over in silence, no longer arises. Once again, the Church finds herself at a disadvantage, and can easily be accused of being out of date when testifying to the divinity of Christ and the reality of the mystery of the Incarnation. The fact is that at present Christ is being proclaimed to the majority of people more from outside the Churches than by the Churches themselves, but a new image of Christ is being imposed, supplanting the one to which the Church bears witness. Christians are bewildered by this. And undeniably it takes some courage today to affirm that Christ is God, since to affirm this is no longer to contradict an affirmation to the contrary, but merely seems an anachronistic statement quite unacceptable to the modern mind. For this image of Jesus to be popularised may be a step towards the discovery of Christ as Son of God, but it can equally well be an obstacle to any intensification of the search. God alone knows! But be that as it may, this attraction to the person of Jesus should make us face up afresh to our responsibilities and to the obligations of our faith. What should Jesus be for us?

On this matter I ask two fundamental questions. First of all, how are we to conceive of our life of faith and how are we to maintain and keep it lively? This is the first question which I propose to discuss.

The second question will lead us to ask how the presence of Jesus is to reveal itself in every aspect of our lives: in sharing the lot of the poor, in the concept of human life and the world of labour which we ought to develop, in participating in political activity or ideological conflict. What is our role to be in all this as religious consecrated to Christ?

Our vocation compels us to share the aspirations and struggles of the people among whom our lot has been cast. That their struggles will most of the time be taken over by some ideology or other is a fact and cannot be otherwise. This is one of our basic problems, and one of our more recent Chapters defined the Fraternity's role in the struggle for social justice and political liberation. At the same time, the Chapter insisted that evangelism must always take first place, that being the Fraternity's essential mission. This mission requires that we accept to be nothing less than prophets of Christ. We must not be afraid of the word 'prophecy'. For our vocation of its very nature puts us at the heart of this problem. Living in the presence of the invisible world, insisting that we are citizens of this invisible world by faith, being aware that by baptism Christ lives in us, that we have to witness to a living Christ and not merely deliver his message, that we have to advance as we live towards the encounter with God: all this might lead us to avoid too much involvement with men or to consider this involvement as being a secondary aspect of our vocation, thus prompting us to live out Christ's silent presence within us in protracted isolation. Now, by virtue of our vocation, we are bound to take human preoccupations seriously. Very true! But if we do take human preoccupations seriously, if we share the lives, the living and working conditions, of the poor, we can easily reach a point where we have hardly any time avaialble for protracted prayer, for theological reading or for meditating on the Word of God. We shall live on our

spiritual capital – for a while. Can we depend exclusively on
the help of the Holy Spirit? Placed like this, can we, in spite of
all, go on being Christ's reflection among men? Can we be the
ones who by their attitudes show what Christ's reactions are
to human affairs? And shall we be free of contamination by
materialistic ideas? Can our loyalty to Jesus remain un-
affected? Isn't there a danger that our loyalty to him will
gradually change into mere loyalty of behaviour at the level of
unselfish love for our brother-men, in the quest for justice,
and in a total devoting of our activities to others? Yes, of
course, for some time at least, we shall go on feeling some
need for contemplation, not without the risk, however, of this
being no more than a natural need felt by everyone from time
to time to stop, draw breath and think in peace. But are we
then still talking about the need for a free and loving encounter with Jesus, with our God: the desire to talk to him
privately and at that moment to forget about effectiveness and
usefulness, because we belong entirely to the Beloved? How
long is this going to go on meaning something to us? For love
is free, and in a sense involves a disregard for effectiveness.
Love is not useful. This is true of the deepest form of human
love, of friendship. Love is sufficient to itself. I do not use my
friend. I do not make use of Christ's message to save men, I
love Christ. In our lives, in our way of living, of working, of
talking and of sharing human leisure, isn't there something
else, bearing witness to another dimension of life, to the fact
that death does have a meaning, that suffering has a meaning,
in the Crucified yet Risen Christ? Sometimes I fear that in this
craze – for it is a craze, make no mistake about it – for sharing
in the human struggle and the task of self-liberation, people
come to forget that anyone representing Christ should be particularly available to the suffering and the dying, to those in a
word who are no more use where political conflict is concerned.

Consider the life of Brother Charles, for he is at the root of
our vocation. He lived in intimate contact with Jesus, not to
make use of it but out of pure need to love. Intimacy with God
in prayer cannot be subordinated to anything other than the
free action of love. Brother Charles said this over and over
again, he proved it, he spent hours and whole nights here, in
this chapel; and this vital activity was not productive of any

apparent result. It has no use at all, other than being absorbed in love for Christ and God. I do not mean to say that intercessory prayer and loving supplication when truly directed to the heart of the Creator and Lord of all things are without results in history. What I do mean is that the motive we have for drawing near to the Lord and giving him our time can be no other than pure love – not a reflex action because we feel the need to have our spiritual batteries recharged. The moment you begin praying because you want to recover a little inner peace and recoup your energy, you have already shifted the focal point of your love and are no longer in the position to be a genuine prophet of Christ. Many overworked business-men, political activists, scientists, may well feel the need, quite apart from any considerations of faith in Christ, to refuel themselves spiritually or morally. To call this a contemplative's need would be nothing if not glib.

Another thing I obseve about Father de Foucauld is that this completely disinterested contemplation transformed his heart, so that in his fellow-men's eyes he really did become a man of God. When someone has become so fixed in intimacy with God that his feelings, outlook and behaviour are profoundly changed, he really does become a man of God for his contemporaries, who see him as called to utter prophetic judgement on human affairs. Brother Charles was recognised as a man of God here at Béni Abbès by everyone living round about and later, too, by the Touaregs in the Hoggar. And although he was obliged to concern himself with temporal affairs and to intervene in the Touaregs' political problems, this was never to the detriment of being a man of God, but very obviously *because* he was a prophet.

That is what I see in Father de Foucauld. And by the light of his example, we have to decide whether it is possible for ourselves to aspire to being men of God, entirely absorbed in the invisible world; and whether, at the same time, while staying faithful to our friendship with Christ, we can labour level-headedly at human affairs and, to put the matter shortly, at the liberation of man in the political sphere.

Here I may say something by way of general introduction. We are by nature not only susceptible to the influence of our environment; in a certain sense we are entirely dependent on it. We must realise this. It is an inescapable condition of being human. Human beings do not exist in isolation. As regards our knowledge of the actual world, whether it be scientific knowledge or any other kind of knowledge which we acquire, whether it be in the forming of our mind, of our criteria of judgment, of the way we think or the way we act, we are not independent, however much we may claim to be so. No one, not even a genius, can lay claim to total independence. We are the creatures of our environment, we are what our environment has made us. You need only consult your personal experience to see how true this is. I would even go so far as to say that we are conditioned by the environment. You know what a strong and virtually indelible mark is left on an individual by his early upbringing and background, by the education he receives, by the way his mind has been trained, by the studies which have taken pride of place and of course by the company he has kept. And this is also true of religion and the way we express our faith. Yes, even for the faith, we are dependent on our environment. We can't do anything about it. You only have to look around you. Why were you brought up a Christian? Why are the village-children over there Moslems? Because of your and their environment. So naturally people talk about traditional religion. How can you expect anything else? For come what may, tradition will make you into something or other, depending on your original environment: either you will be a materialist, or a Moslem, or a Christian, or a Marxist. You cannot be neutral. There is no such thing. Families who claim to bring up their children in total freedom and give them no religious or ideological instruction, on the pretext that they will make their own choice at the age of eighteen, are completely deluded. For the children will be nonetheless conditioned by the various environments which they frequent and by the teaching which they receive. The Church knows this perfectly well. And this is why she exists as the environment in which the faith can be handed down from age to age. To ignore the Church as an institution would amount to saying that the faith has no need of an environment favourable to its propagation and extension. Which is absurd. Without the right kind of environment, the faith would soon stop being handed on and would stop being firm and real, becoming in-

stead little more than the vague content of subjective encounters with God.

Yet we now question the value of and need for an environment – in the name of freedom! But in this respect you will
never in fact be free, and the only freedom you have is that of
choosing which environment to have, not of doing without
one! You cannot escape from one environment without falling
into another one. Whether we are preoccupied with error or
with truth, these are transmitted through environment. Marx-
ists are well aware of this. That is why communist
governments exercise absolute control over schooling, press
and book-publishing. They know that if they are to stamp
their mark on the minds of a generation, the children have to
be immersed from the earliest age in an environment conditioned by socialist ideology. They know that the only way to
mould their minds to the pattern they want is by the influence
of the social environment. Yet we challenge the Church's right
to do the same thing. Once again, true freedom consists, not in
doing without the environment, but in being able to choose
the environments we prefer.

In the past, the Church used to act as communist
governments do today, that is to say by exercising a censorship over books. There is not in fact a single marxist country in which there is complete freedom of publication, whereas
the Church, bowing to the pressure in favour of freedom, has
had to give up her censorship, known as the Index. We all
know how stormily the Church is criticised when she raises
her voice from time to time in judgment on this or that doctrine. The consequences are easy to foresee. The environment
essential to the vitality of the faith is endangered. So we can
ask ourselves another question: Once we admit our
dependence on environment, don't we have a duty deliberately to choose that environment most favourable to the development and strengthening of the life of faith and the flourishing
of our vocation, in so far as the choice lies with us? It would be
a mistake to suppose yourselves invulnerable and to imagine
that as Christians or as religious you can manage without an
environment. This would be completely contrary to the laws
of human nature. Even the Incarnate Word, when wishing to
pass on his message to the world, became subject to the law of
environment. That is why Christ grouped his apostles into a

community with other responsible believers. The earliest Christian community was the environment in which the faith of the first disciples came to fruition. Today, many Christians are confusedly rediscovering this law and once more feel the need to form Christian communities. They realise that, on their own and outside a community environment, they are incapable of receiving the faith, nurturing it and putting it truly into practice.

And we too should consider how we stand. Are we convinced that the faith cannot normally flourish except in a favourable environment, and that this favourable environment is the Church? The Church is the place of God's Word, where it is interpreted and where it is handed on. The Church, you may say, embraces the totality of lights gained and progress made in the faith throughout the successive Christian generations. Here, in the Church, all the quests, intuitions and lights received converge to produce an environment as unique as irreplaceable.

Are you aware of what is needed for your faith to stay lively? Christ's presence within you, which you feel you possess now – are you capable of keeping that faithfully on your own, by the sole fact of having made a resolution to be generous-hearted? No. This is not enough. Your way of leading your religious life will have to include elements which cannot be dispensed with and which themselves are more than means to an end, being structural elements of your very existence. The means may, at a pinch, be dispensed with; they can be altered. But you cannot either choose or alter the essential elements of Christian or religious life. Of these elements, we might cite first a regular study of the Word of God. Nor do I mean that this study of the Word should be confined to the meagre lights of personal interpretation, even when enriched by those of our brothers in the exchange of ideas arising from private Bible-reading sessions. To be sure, the Holy Spirit may grant us valuable insights on these occasions, and these exchanges have their uses. But the Holy Spirit does not dispense us from the law of environment, above all the environment of the Church. What doctor, what marxist, what professional person would pretend that by private reflection and an exchange of ideas with two or three of his colleagues, he could so extend his knowledge and his talents as to be able to do without the masters of the past? Where knowledge is concerned – even knowledge of the Word of God – we must not forget that God has been revealing himself throughout centuries of history and reflection. There is too much at stake for us to be content with superficial answers to our questions. The reality of God is too inexhaustibly immense to be the object of individual personal experience; our own inevitably limited meditations cannot do without fertilisation from outside.

There is a way of limiting ourselves to spontaneity, which is in effect a refusal to accept help from others. Hence the vital importance of study. We cannot do without reading and study. I sometimes wonder whether some of our brothers who are seriously committed to a given environment, pressing in and permeating them from all directions by visits, professional surroundings, television, daily papers, political discussions often supplemented by reading on relevant topics, realise to what an extent they become dependent on this environment, moulding and gradually changing them unawares. What will you be like in a few years' time? Your selflessness will not be in doubt, nor will the rightness of your intentions. But you will have forgotten that you too, like other men, are subject to the laws of human nature, and these you cannot break with impunity. Ask youself what a teacher would be like who never read a new book on his subject. After two or three years, his lessons would be as repetitious as they would be threadbare. Do you think a doctor would stay competent and true to the demands of his profession, were he not to keep himself up to date by reading the medical reviews? If he starts reading literary magazines or publications on quite different topics, it won't be long before he becomes a very incompetent doctor.

Given our life devoted to Christ and Christ's service, aren't we too obliged to be properly informed about the things of God? And can this competence which other people have a right to expect of us be maintained except by reading, study and reflection? I don't think it can. If the life of Nazareth and loyalty to our vocation involve us deeply in the cares and outlook of a given environment, we must assess the effects and dangers likely to ensue. A Little Brother living among sailors may in the course of twenty years become a real sailor, but is it enough for him just to have become a sailor? What is the point of that, if he has not become a genuine witness to Jesus among sailors? That is the question. Your religious life will not have any meaning if, in communion with the Church, you are not Christ's prophet among the people to whom the Fraternity has sent you in God's name. I might put it like this: your vocation requires that you be the product of two environments. And this is precisely why your life will be a hard one. Be humble and clear-headed enough to realise that spending your daily lives with people whose horizons are limited to the struggles of politics or trade-unions and to ideological discussion is bound to have an effect on you in the end. Jesus warned us about this: we cannot simultaneously serve two masters.[13] In this saying of Christ's there is both a nugget of plain commonsense and a serious warning when those two masters happen to be called God and Money. To be sure, you can do several things at the same time and have more than one centre of interest in your life. But you cannot simultaneously devote yourself to two absolutes. God is an absolute, he will not be content with only part of you. Jesus cannot just be one friend among many, a private preoccupation added to a life otherwise totally concerned with and dominated by the things comprising everyday life, even the life of the poor. You cannot have two interests claiming primacy, or devote your life to two absolutes at once. Either it will be God, Jesus, with all the consequences of belonging to him – a life led without fear or favour as concerns yourself as also in service of your fellow-man; or it will be an exclusive preoccupation with political liberation, in which case you will end up a militant. We have to choose one or other of these vocations. We have to make sure that the primacy always remains with Jesus Christ, without letting ourselves be blindly deluded into thinking that we can stay faithful to our mission by living just as we please, without bothering about nourishing our minds, by letting ourselves be swept along by whatever current of thought happens to be flowing, and by being satisfied with adorning the surface of a life thus led with a few moments spent meditating on the Gospel and a second or two of prayer now and then. This is not the way to be an effective witness to Christ among men.

When we held our regional conference in Africa, we invited an African priest to come and share our deliberations. His main contribution was to talk about African religious sensibility. He reproached the western missionaries who had brought the Gospel to his country with not having behaved in a completely religious manner: they were faithful, he said, to their religious exercises but, apart from this, acted, thought and behaved like other people. This gave us food for thought and we were obliged to admit that what he said was true. You will not be a religious consecrated to Jesus if, though faithful to your Gospel meditation, to your minute or two of prayer and your periodical re-examination of what you and the other members of your fraternity are doing, you live for the rest of the time exactly like the working-people around you, sharing their attitudes of mind and working just as they do. I ask you: how deeply, in this case, is your life likely to be permeated by constant pre-occupation with Jesus? I don't think the situation could last for long. Someone has to be the master of your life. Who is it? Do you know? Is it to be Jesus and his Gospel? The Church and the Fraternity? Or is it to be temporal team-activity, taking part in a trade-union struggle or even serving some ideology or other? Let us stay in no doubt about this. Otherwise we may end up as surface-religious, as Little Brothers merely by virtue of membership in a fraternity. We must be clear about this.

And this prompts us to ask another question: Is the environment and atmosphere of the Fraternity sufficient to keep our faith bright? For the Fraternity should be a privileged environment for you. The environment of the Fraternity taken as a whole, the environment of the brotherly community which forms the Fraternity to which you belong, the friendship of your brothers, the mutual trust, prayer and the various activities performed together, are intended to let your vocation develop to the full. But what about the Fraternity environment? What does that consist of? It has to have the depth and relevance characteristic of a Church-environment: for the Fraternity is part of the Body of Christ. The Fraternity does not merely comprise living together and generating enough fellow-feeling to help one another and exchange views from time to time. But I don't want to go into details over this, since you are faced with the fundamental question which you would now do well to consider: Does the Fraternity, your fraternity, really offer you a favourable environment for your religious life as a disciple of Brother Charles of Jesus?

This is a question which you must honestly ask. In any fraternity there are bound to be difficulties, and the brothers will tell you, 'We haven't got time to pray!' My answer to them is, 'There's more to it than that. If you had all the time in the world for prayer, that still wouldn't be enough!' And what about nourishing your faith? Where will you be in a little while? You may well find God gradually becoming remote and alien to you. No longer living by or with God, you won't know how to talk about him. You won't be *a man of God* any more. People don't seek out a man of God, expecting him to be an expert on politics or industrial relations. They want him to talk about the Lord. Even if I do not ask him about the Lord, that is what I expect to hear from him. And some day or other I shall probably need to open my heart to him, perhaps I shall want him to talk to me about Jesus or teach me to pray. And I shall talk to him, to this brother, about this, since I shall feel that he is a man of God. If Moussa, the *amenokal* of the Hoggar used to unburden himself at length to Brother Charles and ask his advice at every turn, it was because he knew him to be a man of God.

It is time to stop. Now, I know that you are not destined to become professors of theology or teachers of Biblical exegesis. And besides, you are vowed to a certain poverty of life. Yet you are destined – and this is true for all of you – to be messengers of Jesus Christ and prophets of his Gospel. You must therefore take all normal means for becoming this and staying this: by taking your study-periods very seriously and by keeping your knowledge abreast of the times. You must live in conditions which enable you to keep your faith so absolute and lively that it governs your life in every particular. First, you must be faithful to prayer – this goes without saying. Next is the regular practice of intelligent, serious-minded Scriptural meditation. You will also have to keep your spirituality and theology up to the mark, so that whatever you have to do will be centred on God. These are the elements on which your life as a *Little Brother of the Gospel* will be based. I am not going to talk about the means to this end now, since it is up to one and all of you to make these elements a permanent feature of your life; the means however may vary according to circumstance.

You must pay particular attention, however hard this may be, to the Church's doctrinal pronouncements. You must therefore be at pains to understand these. Last of all, do not imagine yourselves invulnerable to the eroding effects – despite your own intentions – of reading matter, plays, films and attitudes of mind prevalent in the environment at large. No one is invulnerable. Your deepest held convictions can be gradually, imperceptibly altered by the environment. Hence the need for discipline in your spiritual life, for evaluating the influences at work on you, so that you are not carried away by every wind of doctrine. We cannot dispense with a basic philosophic position from which to judge this ideology or that. Otherwise we shall find ourselves being moulded by them and our faith losing its conviction and growing so dim as no longer to be able to guide our course of action.

In conclusion, I should like to remind you about being faithful to the Eucharist. The way we behave towards the Eucharist constitutes a true test of the state of our faith. If our faith is vacillating and vague, our attitude to the Eucharist will also be vacillating and vague. To the human eye, the consecrated bread and wine appear to be no more than symbols. Why then, beyond these very humble and ordinary appearances, do we attain the mystery of the Real Presence? Because our faith is real. We must not be afraid of being admitted by faith into the real world of God. I know perfectly well that the reality is challenged in the world today. The way some Christians behave towards the Eucharist is the natural result of the vagueness and lack of certainty in their faith. It could hardly be otherwise. And this is why our own attitude to the Eucharist is at once source, test and essential element of our relationship with Christ, living and ever present in our lives.

I say no more. I have not gone into the question of means, since these being practical and concrete have to keep being re-thought as new situations arise. But – and here again I must insist – as regards the elements of your religious life already discussed, you cannot allow yourselves to be negligent about these for long without risking the ruin of your faith.

IV

In Communion with Christ, Liberator from Death and all Evil

We shall continue our reflections on giving our lives to Christ so that he can go on living and extending his mission through us – restrictedly enough, to be sure, owing to our limitations, and despite the obstacles that we put in his way.

We must now talk about Jesus, about his way of being a man, about what he was, about the state he chose or rather the state which was appropriate to his mission and to his being the Son of God and the Incarnate Word. For the human face of Christ and his behaviour on earth have great significance for us: I mean, God's revelation of himself in Jesus, whom we must contemplate as we know him. We cannot conceive of Jesus in any other way. He was sent to us, and what he was he was by force of being the Word of God, Creator of all things, Eternal Son of the Father. We contemplate the Word translated into human mind, heart, feelings, will: and this is Jesus, one unitary person.

If such mysterious identity can occur between God and man, in which the destiny of all mankind and each individual is fulfilled, may we not say that Christ exemplifies the adaptation of human nature to the very being of God? Being the Word of God conditions Christ's way of being a man: his chastity, his supreme detachment from all created things – I mean his poverty – and lastly his obedience to the Father's design, filial obedience, painful though completely clear-sighted, completely responsible, completely willing obedience. Christ's way of being a man – he the first-born of the dead – prefigures what mankind one day will be. Having conquered death, Jesus appeared before his Father in a state of chastity, poverty and total abandonment to the Father's will, thus in a state to be glorified, to be man exalted to the right hand of God. And this is what we must contemplate, given that we believe that it is neither a dream nor empty idealism to claim that we have been called to lead his life here-below, hardships and obstacles notwithstanding, so that we too may achieve Christ's state, may share it, may play our part in it, distantly admittedly but in fact. When the Second Vatican Council spoke about the religious life, it laid greater stress than has ever been done before on the glorious prefiguration of man, represented by the religious state.

All the same, to see the way religious live, you would never guess it! All you see are a few poor wretches, indistinguishable from other people, all of them with failings and problems! Christ's state, which they have chose, if no longer quickened by immense love and by contemplation of a mystery giving it soul and inner vitality, is in itself of no avail. If I do not possess Christ in contemplation, my religious life loses its quality, becomes material observance; chastity becomes no more than celibacy endured as well as may be, with all the defects commonly attaching to this particular predicament; poverty soon turns into endless discussions on economics, on class, on a preference for one kind of poverty rather than another. As for obedience, the very meaning of the word is forgotten! Is it simply acceptance of responsibility for decisions taken in common regarding community life and activity? Here we witness what amounts to the breakdown of religious life, where soul, unity and depth of purpose have been lost. Is it inevitable that such degradation should occur? You can tell from your own experience, from that of the brotherhood of common life to which you belong, and you can also see what happens in other religious orders. Don't let us entertain any illusions on this score. The Church is not offering you an easy ideal, and I cannot present the facts to you other than they are. Look at Brother Charles contemplating and drawing life from the mystery of Christ, look at all the saints: that is what your ideal should be. Even today, whatever the cultural upheavals and crises in civilisation which we are living through, the most important thing for you to do is to bind yourselves tightly to the mystery of the living Christ. Otherwise, your religious life will soon be reduced to a group of people merely living together because of some job to be done, obliged to maintain a modicum of discipline for the sake of getting on with one another and making communal life tolerable. You end up with no more than a legalistic, canonical definition of the religious state. Attaching full weight to our words, we may say that the religious life cannot endure or bear fruit unless rooted in habitual contemplation of Jesus Christ. Otherwise, you will find yourself trying to justify your attitudes and actions one by one – even to yourself – with very unconvincing reasons.

Now, of course the religious ideal when understood as a sharing in Christ's human nature is utopian, in the sense that we shall never be capable or worthy of achieving this, since our configuration to Christ will never be complete. We shall always fall short. Is our concept of religious life then merely an ideal? Well, yes – in a way. But we cannot do without the ideal and we must always keep it before our eyes. A religious ideal often assumes flesh in an immediate, concrete way in the person of a man of God or of a founder: as Brother Charles is for us.

Was he unrealistic? If so, Christ was before him! For Christ it is who bids us follow him this way! Yes, it is unrealistic in the sense that the demands made by this way of life are far beyond our actual condition, with all our actual faults, our actual inadequacies, our actual self-absorbtion. This coming out of ourselves to reach a state which is Christ's is the very opposite of our natural tendency to retreat further into ourselves.

This is why, if in our religious life we lack that strength of prayer, that contemplation nourished by faith and meditation on the things of God, nourished also by sharing the experiences of the saints who have gone before us, that life will be mediocre; it will tend to material observance and merely be a sort of exterior form of life, meaningless and unattractive. And then we shall no longer be able to convey its relevance to other people. For it is by the way I lead my life in religion that I bear witness that it does have meaning. An existence of the exterior sort, even if led with the best will in the world, has no meaning for those who do not believe in the divinity of Christ – except perhaps in such features as its devoted, humble service for the poor; but this is not a distinguishing characteristic in any case, since the monopoly of open-hearted service certainly does not lie with the religious.

The vocation, thus giving me to Christ, at the same time gives me to his mission and obliges me to cooperate with him. For there is a sort of identity between what Christ was within himself, I mean his way of being a man, and the way he discharged his mission. His mission was to be the Incarnate Son and, by virtue of this, the Saviour of men. But what does this mean? What is Christ's mission, in which the Church shares and which it prolongs, Christ's mission in which all Christians are bound to collaborate, this mission discharged in so many different ways by means of all sorts of gifts, ministries and jobs to be done? It is a mission not expressed in a single way but in all sorts of ways by means of differing forms of religious and consecrated life, so much so indeed that what I am about to say will not cover every form of religious life but only yours, the one outlined and practised by Brother Charles so that he too might be a saviour with Jesus.

Yes, what is this mission as Saviour? How is Jesus the Saviour? For if in time past the Christian imagination seized on the image of the Sacred Heart as supreme symbol of Jesus as Saviour of men, we are not so sure today what to think about his role as Saviour. And here I put myself in the world-context in which you yourselves will be living, in the climate of theological speculation, in the mental attitude of Christianity today.

If we accept the unadulterated Gospel, the Gospel as it stands, and if we want to find out what Jesus understood his mission to be, we shall find that it was something overwhelmingly simple, although that simplicity concealed a great mystery, which we cannot understand although Christ lived it out. His mission embraced everything already stated symbolically throughout the range of prophecies foretelling the coming of an universal Kingdom of righteousness and peace. Christ was to acquire this Kingdom by his death. The whole Gospel shows us, through Christ's sayings, that he was travelling towards the Cross and the supreme consummation of that mission. '*It was precisely for this moment that I came*',[14] he was to say one day on realising how fast that hour was coming, as the passing months, soon to be only weeks, brought him nearer and nearer to the Passion. '*It was precisely for this moment that I came*'. And yet he was frightened all the same! These days, we are not anxious to sound the mysterious abyss of suffering into which Christ's Heart would have to plunge. We find this harsh and bewildering, and we tend to elude Christ's mission and pass over this painful aspect of death in silence. What can the significance of the Passion possibly be in the Father's eyes?

Christ's mission is also to proclaim the Gospel. '*I have reveal-ed your name to men,*' he was to say one day when addressing the Father; which is the same thing as saying that he had revealed the secret of the Person of the Father: he had revealed that the Name would forever remain mysterious. Which also means the same thing as revealing to man man's new dignity as son of God, loved with loving compassion, reconciled to his Father and redeemed. But what do we mean by *redeemed*? What has happened between God and man? At first sight, there does not seem to have been any basic change in human behaviour as a result of Christ's Passion or of his self-revelation as God, or of the promulgation of the law of love. After Christ, man gives every appearance of behaving exactly ss he did before Christ. And yet, when Jesus draws near to men, to the poor, to sinners, to the sick, and when he forgives or heals them, he often adds, '*Go, your faith has saved you!* . . . *Go, and sin no more!*' From what and how has this man been saved? – '*Sin no more!*' – Jesus was under no illusions about human nature, he knew perfectly well that the man was incapable of avoiding relapsing into sin. What did he mean, then?

Christ's mission is also its ending. Beyond the terrestrial phase, Christ's destiny is fulfilled by his glorification. The glorification is the goal of his mission, since this concerns men too. Jesus desired this most intensely. '*Father, it is time for you to glorify me with that glory which I had with you before ever the world was*'.[15] He knew himself to be the Son of God, but the man he was had first to pass through the fires of suffering, the baptism of the Cross and death, to enter Life and to be transfigured by the Father's glory.[16] the baptism of death, mysteriously necessary before he could enter the Resurrection state, which is no longer of the earth. Hence the fleeting, mysterious quality of the apparitions of the Resurrected Christ, of the Son clad in the glory of his Father. Those apparitions of Christ were certainly *real*, but their reality was no longer of this earth. The Glorified Christ no longer belonged to the world of his apostles, he could not belong to the world anymore, he belonged to another world. Yet it was certainly he, and not another! He had to convince his disciples of the bond necessarily existing between his death and his present state, and this was why he showed them the wounds in his hands and the scar left by the spear. He also had to convince them that, beyond the infinite distance separating those two worlds, he was still the same person, not someone else; that they were not seeing a ghost or an illusion; and that what he had told them about eternal life and the resurrection of the dead was true and had come true, first for him, and later would, with him, for the men whom he now called his brothers.[17]

Such is the breadth of Christ's mission. But the only part of it which Christ wants to prolong through us and share with us is primarily what he was doing in his terrestrial condition – which is the same as ours – as prophet, evangelist and priest crucified by love.

Even if it means going into some detail, we shall have to clarify this notion of salvation, for there is still much mysterious about it for us. All the more necessary too, since today it is the subject of discussion and is understood in various different ways. What then is human salvation? Our first reaction will be to ask: But does man need to be saved? What does he need to be saved from? If I refer to the catechism as taught at the beginning of the century, I find very precise ideas about this. The conditions in which human salvation was to be achieved were set out in so clear and orderly a fashion that there were no loose ends at all. Immediately after death, the soul received its individual judgment, as a result of which it went to purgatory or hell, or less probably straight to heaven; for it seemed virtually impossible in a period still to some extent influenced by Jansenism for a soul to go to heaven without first undergoing purification. Then came the wait for universal judgment linked to the resurrection of the body and eternal retribution.[18] This was all perfectly straightforward! Being saved by the grace of Jesus Christ and the mercy of the Father consisted in avoiding eternal damnation. Venial sin was what deserved a punitive stint in purgatory, and mortal sin earned hell since it implied a deliberate rejection of God. To most Christians, as a result, heaven seemed inaccessible except after a long time spent in purgatory. There was a tendency to believe that the number of the elect was very small. In any case, going to heaven was only possible because Jesus had opened the gate by his Passion and Death. That's what salvation was. The capacity thus offered us for enjoying the vision of God constituted the ultimate end of our redemption by Jesus. We cannot see God unless we are his sons, since the beatific vision entails admission to the intimate life of the Trinity, which in turn presupposes a filial relationship and hence participation in the vision which Jesus Christ the Son has of the Father.

As set out in the catechism, this account of salvation, precise, often imagistic, sometimes narrow and somewhat rigid owing to Jansenistic influences, though basically accurate, produces hostile reactions nowadays. This concept is not really acceptable to the modern mind. Hence, many Christians today tend to minimise the vision and gravity of Judgment Day in the assurance of having been forgiven by Jesus. Man is already saved from sin and its effects. Hence, a certain indifference towards faults, especially those that cause no harm to our neighbour. People argue that if God created men, he did not do this to damn them; that if he really is the Father which the parable of the Prodigal Son represents him as being, he cannot but bring all men to everlasting bliss. There is a weakening awareness of the demands of holiness in human life and a certain relaxing of conscience on several scores. Modern spirituality lays stress on our being already risen with Christ and on all things being already accomplished. We are sons of God, and Jesus gives us that eternal life which we already have within us. As for what used to be called 'the last things', I mean judgment after death, the nature of our survival, the vision of purgatory, or what Jesus called '*the outer darkness*', people spend little time thinking about these. They are not relevant.

In one way, there is something healthy and positive in this refusal to investigate a mystery which is probably impenetrable in any case and about which Christ himself had little to say. And besides, the present state of the world has produced an increased awareness of our responsibility as regards a number of types of social injustice: which responsibility, it must be admitted, the Church and majority of Christians had not sufficiently grasped hitherto. Hence today's somewhat different concept of evil and the sense of urgency over human liberation. And hence the tendency, in the throes of social and political conflict, to interpret salvation in Jesus Christ as meaning an immediate liberation, to be achieved by means of social and political conflict. This concept tends to be exclusive of others, not necessarily denying but forcing the notion of individual eternal salvation into the background as though it were of secondary importance.

The saints – and here I mean those men who have lived Christ's charity to the full – have always shown an intense desire to relieve mankind of every sort of misery and suffering and to do battle against evil and injustice. And this is verifiable for all periods throughout history. But today the liberating project has taken on cosmic dimensions – a political design to liberate the entire human race from evil. This is a task in which all men of good-will feel bidden to take part. What is the Christian's place and his specific task? Jesus, surely, is the prime mover of this liberating work. Isn't he the liberator from all oppression, from all injustice, from all suffering caused by selfishness, ill-will, ignorance, incompetence and indifference? No one would deny the positive good in our discovery of these new demands of charity towards men. But how does salvation in Jesus Christ fit into this? Does it still lie in the mystery of individual destiny which we refuse to investigate? In that supreme liberation from *the outer darkness*, about which we have apparently nothing to say and for which we do not really know how to prepare? Shouldn't we regard eternal salvation as a product of the universal, open-hearted love evinced by us for our fellow-men and of all the immediate improvements thus achieved?

There is however one question still to be answered, fundamental to today's point of view and also to the Christian's faith: What is the significance of the world, of its future, of its history, in the perspectives of eternal life, of the resurrection of the dead and of that mysterious prospect of a new earth and a new heaven? Contemporary ideologies represent the earthly salvation of mankind as the only possible absolute and only realistic end envisageable for man. And the ideologies derive their effectiveness and dynamism from this very conviction. Yet a concept of this sort obliges us to regard mankind itself as an absolute, as a supreme reality. But what is mankind, taken all in all? Isn't each individual a parcel of mankind? Mankind can only be the totality of living people. To erect Mankind as such on a world peopled with graveyards makes no sense. Individuals, peoples, nations, cultural communities together make up mankind as existing at any given moment of world history. What is the future as such of mankind, regarded as something independent of or superior to the people composing it? Once the individuals have died, what is left of your Mankind? There will be no Mankind in the future, if the world comes to an end. Admittedly, the possibility that history may stop is not one of our principal worries since the more immense the vistas of prehistory and evolution afforded us by science, the more conscious we feel of this prodigious time-span and the less we think about how, when and whether it will end. The duration of things defies imagination and for the majority of people has virtually come to be identified with eternity itself. Once you begin measuring space by millions and millions of millions of light-years, language itself and notions of futurity all go into the melting-pot. People are no longer interested in eschatology. The only compelling reality is history.

Yet God knows how short life is! It is almost embarrssing to state such a well-worn truth! Compared with the host of previous generations and the length so far of the history of the world, what does the length of our own existence amount to? As far as we individually are concerned, the history of the world will soon be over! Memorised experience was what gave man the power to dominate the ages through which our species was slowly emerging into history. Each individual thus encapsulates the history of the race. About eternal salvation we can know nothing except by faith. We can only listen to what Jesus thought fit to reveal to us about it, to what the Church received from him to pass on to us, to what the community of the faithful has always believed. Now, what we know by these means, what the Church and community of the faithful have attested, is that man does have an eternal future in the coming Kingdom proclaimed by Jesus. I say man advisedly; I mean all men and each of them. For this eschatological future is open to man as son of God and hence as a free spirit. For the law revealed to him by his Creator is a law of love, and the eternal future offered him depends on a free choice. Man is free to decide whether his life shall blossom in Him who is Love; he can counter love with hatred or indifference, that is to say, reject it. Experience, both personal and historical, teaches us that it is, alas, quite easy to refuse.

For changeable beings like us, of course, this refusal is never final, nor is it ever categoric since our intellects and wills are too limited for us to be capable of such an absolute decision. Refusal, involving the spoiling of our future, is tantamount to a judgment – not because sentence will be passed by the Sovereign Judge, an idea based on an anthropomorphic conception of God, but because those who refuse to make themselves completely open to love make it impossible for themselves to enjoy the supreme blossoming as sons of God in eternal love later.

When St John of the Cross, one of those who have penetrated most deeply into the mystery of God through prayer, tells us that we shall be judged on love, he is right. It would however be equally true to say that love is what will judge us; for either love will be accessible to us in its infinite fulness or we, not being adapted to it, shall have to turn our backs on it forever. The destiny of a son of God demands no less.

The vision of the mystery of love revealed to us in the Trinity of Persons of the Living God is not only attested to us by faith but by the inner experience to which the Spirit leads countless Christians. The Spirit assures us that we are in the truth, while the entire gospel shows us that Jesus always saw himself in this eschatological light.

We thus grasp how it is that Jesus liberates us, in that he does everything to make our freedom lucid and firm, so that we shall be able to choose love and not the rejection of love. This is what salvation or liberation means. The ultimate purpose of the Saviour's mission is to make us absolutely free, since the freer a man is, the more able he is to love and the more able to choose real love. It is because man is a slave to his own limitations that he is unable to choose real love, even when he feels an unsatisfied thirst for it deep within him. Yes, Jesus liberates us, by the faith and hope he arouses in us, and by the Cross, from the servitude of sin. This servitude is due to our temporary refusal to love, caused by our incapacity, by our paralysis of will or by ignorance. Sin takes on many forms. But whatever the form, it engenders a servitude from which we need to be set free. This setting-free is not something abstract or impersonal; it is something peculiar to each individual, depending on what our inner or outer servitudes may be. These may have their origins in society, in the world, in our mental outlook, our culture, our family; in a word, in our environment, and in whatever habits our surroundings have effectively engrained in us. So we see that liberation in Christ cannot take place in the depth of the heart without an accompanying process of liberation as regards the world as well. Where a number of ideologies go wrong is in limiting their notion of liberation exclusively to that of liberation from social injustice and oppression, whereas there are all sorts of other factors causing servitude, hemming man in and preventing him from achieving his inner liberation.

Above all, Jesus liberates us from death, for no liberation from sin is possible without the destruction of death. Why is this? Because liberation from sin puts us on the road to absolute, and so to eternal, love. We have to be liberated from death, since death puts an end to all our aspirations. What would be the good of aspiring to Love if everything were to be stopped and brought to nothing one day by death? Death mastered, conquered by eternal life, is the greatest liberation of all. Whatever dreams we may have of prolonging man's biological existence, liberation from death can only be the work of God; for it is not merely a matter of stopping this present life from coming to an end, but of transforming its very nature. We are liberated from death by Christ, by going through it and beyond it; for first we have to die as Christ too died. But from this dying, life is born. We die to life on earth to be reborn to an eternal life like his. This is the Paschal mystery.

Liberation from sin and liberation from death are thus connected, for liberation from death presupposes liberation from sin, and liberation from death crowns the life to which liberation from sin has first admitted us. They are also connected in the sense that neither one nor the other can be achieved except at the cost of renunciation and suffering – that scandal of the human condition. Suffering accepted, transcended and made fruitful by the sufferings of the Son of Man becomes a sharing in the life-giving sufferings of Christ.

And here we are faced with something so mysterious that most people do not know what to think about it. Some reject it altogether; others fall back on a purely rational explanation. What does Christ's death mean for us? What is the meaning of Christ's Passion? The fertilisation of human suffering by the sufferings of the Son of Man involves a sort of sanctification of human suffering. Whatever was experienced by the Son of God while in the flesh becomes sacred. Human life is sacred because assumed forever by the Son of God. Man is divine! Divine in his potentialities, divine by virtue of his origin, divine in his aspirations and in his salvation. In Jesus Christ we recognise ourselves. So, when a man is despised, when he is crushed, when a man is rejected by his brothers, it is the Son of Man who is being despised and crushed and rejected. Christ's identity with Everyman, especially with the poor and suffering, is, though mysterious, a living fact. We sometimes give the impression nowadays of being the first people to have made this discovery, although Christians have been acting on it from earliest times. When St Francis of Assisi discovered the mystery of the love of Christ, he felt impelled to get off his horse and kiss the leper coming towards him. Behind the superficial features of this disfigured and unattractive man, he had recognised the face of the Son of Man. And this was the reason why Jesus was subjected to suffering and contempt, as Isaiah had foretold. '*So disfigured did he look that he seemed no longer human . . . he was despised, the lowest of men, a man of pains, familiar with disease, despised and we disregarded him. But they were our diseases he was bearing, our pains that he was carrying . . . The punishment reconciling us had fallen on him and we were healed by his bruises,*'[19]

This mystery of redemptive substitution is very hard to grasp! I do not think in fact that we can ever grasp it, although we may experience it to the full by giving ourselves to Jesus, God's servant suffering for us and because of us. God's holiness and what this exacts are beyond us. We cannot offer a rational explanation for it. God's holiness, our calling to be holy, man's freedom to choose not to be saved: all this is at odds with modern attitudes of mind. To say nothing of the angelic world, or the demons, or the struggle between light and darkness: for many of our contemporaries dismiss all this out of hand. Yes, this is completely beyond us. How then can we understand the wherefore of an atoning sacrifice? How can Christ's sufferings and death be that sacrifice? Why was it necessary? Wasn't Love in itself enough to put everything right?

Given the current concept of man and human evolution, modern scientific thought must inevitably reject the notion of redemption as a myth, as a survival from an outmoded religious system. But that Jesus should have shed his blood for our sins, and that he should have wished his body and blood to remain with us as an invisible sacrifice until the end of the world in the Eucharist, cannot be accidental or out of date. We are well aware that we too have to enter this mystery of blood and suffering if we want to love to the end. But this does not stop us from being appalled at the atoning sacrifice achieved by Christ's Passion, a sacrifice prefigured by that of the paschal lamb and all the burnt-offerings of the Old Covenant and fulfilling the word of Scripture that *'if there is no shedding of blood there is no pardon'*.[20] This really appals us. And yet, let man's reason revolt as it may at the bloody price of his redemption, never has man himself shed so much blood in the world on more diverse ideological pretexts than today. And those who claim to be liberating their fellow-men are the first to shed oceans of blood in this cause. So there is no reason why we, for our part, should not accept this mystery of Christ condemned by us to shed his blood on the cross to liberate us.

Christ's progress towards the cross in fulfilment of his mission has to be understood by us within the all-embracing mystery of his intercession. Between God the Father, Creator thrice Holy, and his beloved but frail, sinful, rebellious, arrogant creature, rises Christ's interceding prayer. Do not let us try to understand. The imagery which people thought fit to use in the past was certainly defective: God is not athirst for blood. He has had more than enough bloody sacrifices. *'I am sick of holocausts of rams; the blood of bulls and goats revolts me'*,[21] the Lord exclaimed through the mouth of Isaiah. Yet was it not He who, through the ministry of Moses, had decreed and regulated that sacrificial ritual prefiguring the blood eventually to be shed as irrefutable sign of the highest form of love that the Son could have for his fellow-man?

Hence we must approach the mystery of Christ's passion and death with an infinite respect for our own lives, for the sufferings which we shall have to face, in ourselves and in our fellow-men, for the liberation from sin to be effective and for the highest form of love to be revealed. For this is how Christ's intercession between God and ourselves bears fruit. But Jesus is not only the intermediary between God and us, for he is himself simultaneously God and one of us. Christ achieves in himself what the very content of evangelisation should be; for this does not merely consist in handing on a message, a teaching recorded in the Gospel, not even a system of wisdom, but in making Jesus Christ himself known in his death, in his life, in his resurrection and in his mystery as Son of God. That is what evangelisation is: the rest, the message of peace and brotherly love flows from it. This is why the apostles proclaimed more, in a sense, than Jesus himself had taught. Jesus had only prepared the way for evangelising, since what he had come to bestow on men could only be acquired by his death. Until he had actually died and risen again, what Jesus was going to achieve could only be proclaimed in metaphor. That is to say, when he happened to talk about these future events to his closest apostles, he could not be and was not understood. His clearest allusions to what would have to happen to him in Jerusalem, where he would have '*to suffer much from the elders, the high-priests and the scribes, and be put to death and, on the third day rise again*',[22] were merely greeted with inattention, incomprehension or scepticism. Nobody listened. And it was just the same when he mentioned the possibility of giving his flesh as food and his blood as drink, to confer eternal life on his disciples and raise them to life on the Last Day: no one would listen and the crowd dispersed in embarrassment. Yet these are the realities of redemption: Jesus given, slaughtered, eaten, his body pierced, his blood poured out, to become the Living Bread.

How does the mystery of death and intercession, personally lived by Jesus, actually affect us? I mean: are we merely the beneficiaries of the sacrifice or are we called to take part in it? By sacrifice I mean the offering of a voluntary death, a death freely accepted for love of men to contribute towards their liberation. Can we envisage our life and death as an actual sharing in Christ's sacrifice and intercession? Are we called to this sort of solidarity with our fellow-men and with Christ? The idea of the solidarity of the People of God and of communal responsibility is very marked throughout the Bible. We are responsible for one another by virtue of those relationships on which the human community is based. And to this natural solidarity, Christ adds a special dimension: the Church, which is his body in a realler sense than we perhaps suppose. Far from diminishing this responsibility, Christ by taking the task of redemption on himself has made it even realler and more essential. And how can we not identify ourselves with Christ the Saviour, and how can he not identify himself with all men, when he comprehends all mankind, suffering, dying, returning to life in him? What respect would Jesus have for our freedom, which means that we are made in God's image, if he were to deny us any responsibility in the essential task of liberating our fellow-men? How could the fruits of redemption be to increase our ability to love, were our freedom not associated with that of Christ, giving his greatest proof of love on the cross?

It is not enough for us to be the beneficiaries of Christ's cross and intercession; we are called to be crucified with him, to be intercessors with him. Here-below in our tormented lives and in our deaths, Christ continues that part of his mission which for him personally is already over, since he cannot suffer anymore or die again.

No one has ever lived this or expressed it more intensely than the Apostle Paul. Read him again. Since the Church first came into existence and there were Christians on this earth, this mystery has been lived out not only by the martyrs but by all disciples of Jesus. This invisible yet real solidarity has become the communion of saints. An incessant exchange of love, merits and prayers, and a single destiny unite all men to one another in the Church, all being sanctified by Christ and members of his body. We depend on one another, since we are all associated with Christ in his sufferings for men, with Christ as he redeems mankind, with Christ as he intercedes with the Father. We are thus involved to the full in a mysterious, invisible activity.

Because we believe that this is so, we must acquire a sense of suffering and a sense of having been called to be perpetual intercessors with Jesus in prayer. It is enough if I remind you here of the dual obligation of our mission. It is for you to find ways of discharging these obligations in your lives. This cannot be done on your own. We constantly need to rediscover the purpose of the state of life to which our religious life specifically consecrates us. Now, the Church tells us that by virtue of our vocation, we religious are specifically consecrated to the things of the Kingdom of God, I mean to activities specifically those of Jesus Christ. Yes, in Christ Crucified we have to discover the meaning of suffering. We have to accept it, not merely because it cannot be avoided, but because no one can live and love without passing that way, because we can only grow in love by being willing to suffer. We have to be prepared to do this. We must not be surprised when we meet suffering, must not be scandalised by it, but must learn to go beyond it by discovering within it the imperative of greater love. Then our sufferings, consecrated by those of Christ and freely offered, become sacrifice. In them we find a hidden efficacity, and hence a meaning. If you are afraid of suffering, you cannot live to the full, since you will have lost the freedom of love without reverse. All selfless love entails painful renunciations, and these have to be freely accepted.

How does suffering redeem? When we see people suffering or when we ourselves are touched by suffering and this is accepted as our share in the sufferings of Crucified Love, in it we discover, painfully, the hard way, in the darkness, a fruitfulness, a call to transcend ourselves. Suffering purifies us, it shows things in their true proportions, it disposes us to seek the absolute, makes us humble, throws us back on God. The fruit of suffering humbly borne is self-abandonment into the hands of God. There is a risk that intense suffering may make us helpless, miserable, isolated, but when it throws us back on Christ it makes us share the weakness of God, which is more powerful than the strength of men.[23]

Suffering is also a way of communicating with others. The experience of the saints teaches us that. In union with the sufferings of Jesus, we become capable of showing mercy, respectful pity and compassion. What consolation are we in a position to offer to people who are suffering? Some sufferings are beyond all human remedy. It is a terrible mistake to imagine that economic or political liberation, or even what is called a reorganisation of society, can eradicate human suffering. This would be an idle and deceptive hope. Men will never cease to suffer in their hearts, in their feelings, in their families, owing to illness, infirmity, the death of loved ones.

The most radical transformation of human society will never succeed in shielding us from sorrow. Christ intervenes at a much deeper level, there where suffering can be rejected. You know this already: sometimes suffering destroys, it can provoke revolt, it may harden us, it may make us bitter towards our fellow-man. But, looking further, we can accept the suffering in our lives as a sharing in Christ's sufferings, offered in union with all the sufferings of mankind: this offering henceforth counts as intercession. But what is intercession? Just talking about it won't satisfy anyone.

Let us look at Jesus. The most perfect, the only true intercession is found in him, for he is the Son. Between him and the Father this free exchange of mutual love and admiration exists pre-eminently: a filial exchange the secret of which is forever hidden from us until that day when we ourselves are able to contemplate the Father with the Son. But even here-below it is given to us to perceive the grace of God in prayer, as a reflection of that silent contemplation of the God of Love inhabiting the soul of Christ. Intercession goes further than this. If we, as sons, have access to the Father, and if we, as free men loyal to one another, have a responsibility towards our fellow-men, must we not, having been created by God in his own image, be associated by him and with him in his supreme activities as Creator and Saviour? This seems self-evident to me – by faith, of course. Everything fits together, in the vision which faith affords us of things. Otherwise, it seems to me that God would be inconsistent in his original intention as Creator. If God has conceived man as a creature with free choice, and if he destines him for that supreme act of freedom, which is to accept his love and respond to it, how could he not accept that willing cooperation from us which is consistent with our dignity as sons? If a filial relationships exists between us and him, it follows that it is possible for us to plead, to ask, in a word, to intercede. But here we encounter an insurmountable obstacle: how can our intercession, taking place in time, be heard, be effective and exert an influence on the course of things, that is, preserve from evil, save from sin, obtain a blessing for others, if everything takes place in accordance with an eternal design or inextricable pattern of necessary causes? If God is infinitely good, how can we suppose that he waits for us to ask before giving men what is best for them? We are now involved in questions which are very hard to answer in terms of rational demonstration! Impossible for us to explain a mystery which has ever baffled the best brains of Christendom: how to reconcile God's creative freedom with man's created freedom. Nonetheless, assured by faith in the teachings of Jesus and thanks to the saints' experience and our own, we know that there really is such a thing as intercession. Faith tells us that prayer is efficacious, thus fully justifying the role of the contemplative in history. Man was saved from his sin, from his rebellion, from his pride, by Christ's intercession culminating in his offering of his very life. Anyone capable of laying down his life proves that he loves, and the efficacity of his intercession is measured by love. The sacrifice consummated in suffering freely offered is in itself an act of intercession. The power of our intercession can never reside in the way we word our plea, however sincerely, nor in peaceful supplication costing us nothing. Intercession must burst forth like a cry from our lives, from the depths of our being, from the depths of our own experienced misery and from our awareness of other people's misfortunes made our own by our own loving soldarity with them. Like Jesus, and in communion with him, our whole existence becomes intercession. And thus our life becomes integrally united in solidarity with men and in continuous intercession with Jesus Christ before the Father.

To conclude, I should like us all to reflect for a little while on the way in which Christ's disciples' intercession can influence the course of history, the life of the Church, the growth of the Kingdom of God and the life of the individual, particularly of those whom we love or those to whom we are bound by special links which give us the right to intercede more insistently for them – a right which God does not ignore. How is it possible for intercession to be efficacious? When we try to answer this, imagination and reason are equally misleading. Nothing I can say can make you understand, but at least I hope to show you that for intercession to have an invisible efficacity is neither absurd nor impossible. This is really all we can say, since the actual fact of intercession cannot be held in doubt as far as we are concerned, given the reality of the communion of saints attested by the practice of the Church: for she, in her members, has never stopped praying from the first moment she came into existence. I confine myself to two observations on the matter.

Exceptional cases apart, it is beyond the scope of our means to know whether our prayers are efficacious or not – which does not, however, mean that they have been in vain. So we have to forgo that satisfaction, and perservere in the faith that we are heard. Prayer does not in some extraordinary way alter the course of events, for its action is situated outside time, our free intervention by prayer having been present at the origin of things in the free act of the Lord and Ordainer of all things. We cannot understand anything about our situation in relationship to God, if we are not capable of at least admitting that we must be situated outside time. Here-below we are doomed to judge things according to the succession of events. The brevity of a human life in relation to time as measured by the cosmos means that cosmic time is completely beyond our power to conceive. But when we have to put outselves outside time altogether. ... In God's eternal present there is a wonderful collaboration between our freedom, our intercession, our acts of love, all the cries rising from mankind to heaven and God's freedom as he creates the world. We might say that man, being eternally present at the act of creation by virtue of his intercession, has by virtue of his freedom, his love or his refusal, in a sense contributed to creating the world and fixing the course of history. What took place in the course of Christ's passion and during Christ's history – for Christ had his history too – up to the moment of his resurrection: all those events, one whole dimension of them, existed outside time. The unfolding of time is inscribed in the eternal present of God. All history – of mankind, even of Christ and the Church – is one immense, single reality already completed in God, though for us it unfolds in the successive moments of our meagre existence. Only a contemplative is able to discern these things in God's light and so glimpse the incomparable value of his own intercessory prayer.

The efficacity of the Church's prayer or of the individual's prayer is neither apparent, nor measurable, nor demonstrable. History unfolds according to God's design and, as we say, our powers of expression being inept, 'according to what has been foreseen by God'. Jesus is the Lord of History. He is the Messiah whose glorious reign will dawn one day, and history's end has no ultimate meaning except in relation to Christ's universal sovereignty.

Such are the basic facts about how we share in Christ's mission, in his mission as Saviour. We do not have to choose between time and eternity, between history and the Kingdom. For there is no breach between these two realities. From the mere fact of being already committed to eternal life by the mystery of Christ, our lives are committed to a universe other than the visible; I mean the divine universe. But for all this, our lives are nonetheless totally involved in human history, in that succession of events of which our little earthly lives are woven and by which they are hemmed in. The effort we have to make is not so much to maintain our commitment to human things, for this we can hardly avoid, being what we are, but to maintain our committment to the divine. This is why I shall have more to say to you about this, for a retreat is the right time for taking stock of such things.

Once you leave this hermitage, your awareness of the invisible will begin to fade: I have no illusions about this. It is perfectly normal. You will have to make an effort to relive what you have learnt in contemplative silence here. You will have to maintain a perpetual cycle, a regular rhythm, of response to sometimes contradictory demands, if you are to keep your life in equilibrium between total commitment to men and equally total commitment to eternal life within you. I prefer the expression 'commitment to men' rather than 'commitment to the world' – God did not love the world as such, but the men living in the world.

By consenting to be religious, you have consented to give your lives up to Christ, for him to imprint them with what was his own state of life. By the same token, he admits you to his own mission. All Christians are intercessors with Christ, all participate in the Eucharist and in Christ's sacrifice, all suffer as sacrificial victims: and, as religious, you particularly so. Not only do you have to pay more attention to the performance of that mission, in particular to intercessory prayer, both as regards the time which you ought to devote to it, as also the importance that intercessory action should have in every aspect of your lives; but intercession should be so much your primary task that you can witness to this and say in all honesty with Brother Charles that your vocation consists in being *a Saviour with Jesus*. Father de Foucauld, like many other contemplatives, was a man of great simplicity of heart. He had no need to be told what his vocation required of him; he did not argue the matter. You will find nothing along that line in his notes or writings. He contemplated, he lived and, as far as he was concerned, that was all there was to it. I do not think we can really live for any ideal until we stop discussing it. The realities by which a man lives are those which he regards as facts. One of the fruits of contemplation is precisely to establish these facts for ourselves: for the facts, though communicated by faith, can only be confirmed as such by our personal experience of God. This is why these facts, fundamental as they are, cannot be passed on to others. Even if I know for a fact that my intercession is truly efficacious, I cannot convey this awareness to my fellow-man or tell him anything to the purpose, for he cannot discover this fact for himself, to the point where his own life bears its imprint, except by his own faith, a faith kept bright by desire and prayer and by his communion with Christ, the perpetual intercessor with the Father.

Here I shall stop. Now you must make your own practical resolutions about the mean which you ought to adopt for you to become and remain true *saviours with Jesus*.

V

Meeting God and our Fellow-Man on the Path of Renunciation

Here are a few thoughts now on how we should respond to the demands of our Christian and religious vocation in ways that Christ, the Church and our fellow-men have a right to expect of us. I shall be discussing this subject in connexion with asceticism and the need for a rule of life.

We are all anxious to enjoy life and to make the most of it. The younger generation, growing up in an increasingly constricting, industrialised, organised and all-providing society, want to enjoy life; and they often let off steam in pretty wild and disorderly ways.

You see, enjoying life is a sign: the sign that we have become the people whom we were meant to be. When Father de Foucauld said that he was infinitely happy and deeply at peace for the simple reason that God was happy, we feel that he had completely fulfilled himself as a human being. People who saw him living in utter destitution may have pitied him for no longer enjoying the pleasures of the world, for having embraced a life of austerity, since the renunciation and privation were the only aspects of his life they could see. How could he feel any satisfaction in living with people of an alien culture, of alien mentality and alien interests? What sort of relationship could he have with them? Yet he was deeply happy. In the same way, the Poor Man of Assisi was a happy man, happy to be alive – so much so that his happiness was one of his most influential qualities. The same might be said of all the saints, whatever their temperament or the way in which their joy expressed itself.

Fear of living, anxiety about tomorrow, the pressures of a complex industrial society, compel man to tragic, inhuman adaptations which destroy the essential qualities of life. Religious life is not exempt from the influence of the environment. Man is extremely fragile; he can easily sustain injury, especially in adolescence, which affects his most secret and intimate self. And yet it is astonishing to observe, beset by so many destructive factors, how resilient, how resistant man is! In spite of all, he is never completely destroyed, discovering new resources in himself to react, to rebuild, or merely to keep afloat on the surface of a partly dehumanised world. Anthropologists maintain that of all animals man possesses the greatest faculty for adapting himself to his environment. But there should be a limit to the use of this faculty; for man has no right to consent to be disfigured. His supreme and incontestable duty is to become as fully human as possible and to adopt the right means to do so.

So it is with our religious vocation: we are not what we ought to be, but we have to become it. Each individual is obliged – or he risks abdicating his true nature – to become what he is, that is, a man in the fullest sense of the word. If he is a Christian, he must become what he is, that is, a disciple of Christ, pledged to being exactly like Christ.

How is this to be done? The need for spontaneity, for freedom, the rejection of all but one's own personal experience, the quest for what is now called authenticity, all characterise contemporary man. He refuses not to be himself. In some countries, this quest for authenticity can actually mean going backwards to a dim and distant past in which the cultural roots of the people are embedded, that is, to a pre-Christian way of life. Elsewhere, the quest for authenticity can take the form of an overriding need for complete freedom of self-expression and experiment, to the exclusion of all moral considerations, these being regarded as taboos, as intolerable, baseless, arbitrary restraints unjustifiably imposed on the way people want to live and love.

You know all this as well as I do. So I shall not go into the matter any further. I merely remind you of the context in which we have to consider the question of salvation in Jesus Christ, which some people tend to regard as salvation achieved, rather than as salvation to be achieved. Under the pressure of ideologies now current, Christians have become alerted to the existence of collective sin productive of serious social consequences, while simultaneously losing the sense of the moral obligations affecting their own personal, private and even family behaviour. I have to admit that I sometimes feel rather uncomfortable even in front of a Christian audience when talking about God's commandments, owing to the indifferent or hostile reactions to which this sort of conception of our relationship to God gives rise. Isn't talk about 'commandments', obligations, prohibitions pronounced by God, as good as saying that we are not capable of deciding for ourselves how we ought to behave, and that to be a full man we must submit to commandments which, even if they do come from God, are unconditionally imposed on us? Now, of course, Jesus Christ has revealed to us that his Father's commandments are in fact only the various expressions of the various requirements of a law of love; so that for anyone prepared to love there is not in fact any constraint, but only sovereign freedom. This freedom however is contained within this love, a prisoner as it were of God's demands. From what constraints then have we been set free and what sort of freedom have we been conceded? Fow we are now Love's prisoners!

Man has a natural tendency to decide how to behave, by using his own judgment and depending on circumstance, without always being able to assess the effects that his conduct may have on other people. And increasingly he claims the right – as the prerogative of his dignity – to decide for himself what his code of conduct and destiny as man should be. Hence the question which now has to be asked: What is man?

Unlike other creatures, we are in fact obliged to ask ourselves this question. For man is not born what he ought to be; he has to shape himself; he can change and evolve. Man trains himself. Now, this is where Christ's demands come in! They are very stringent! '*You must be perfect, just as your heavenly Father is perfect*'.[24] What does this mean? We already know that we fall far short of perfection. The goal to which man should approximate is way beyond him. How then can he grasp the holy requirements of God his Father? In our days, least of all. For the Jews of old, divine holiness was embedded in a tissue of moral obligations, laws and sacred rites engendering the fear of God and developing a sense of what divine holiness exacted. But how were these requirements to be holy to be translated into terms of moral conduct?

The Gospel alone can answer this question as completely as

lies with human beings to answer it. Warning us that we must become holy, as our heavenly Father is holy, Jesus simultaneously offers himself as the only way by which this can be achieved: for, as man, he is holy with all his Father's holiness. If we try and grasp the totality of the demands of what we call the Gospel Law, we shall find the Gospel's portrait of the ideal man – of which Christ is the sole perfect example. Even when incarnate in the person, heart and life of Christ, the many practical demands of the Law of Love will always bewilder us by their vistas of sacrifice and their paradoxical insistence on the blessedness of the poor, of those persecuted for righteousness, of those who suffer, weep and are hungry and thirsty. It is by no means easy to grasp all the dimensions of man as portrayed in Christ. We foresee that, when we set out with him, we are taking a rugged course which in its precepts makes few concessions to reason. At the same time, we know that the demands made by Christ's holiness are exerted at those inner depths where all secrets are revealed, as well as our thirst for truth and love. This often escapes the attention of modern man, all too exclusively concerned with his social and political behaviour. For the secret life and deepest aspirations of my soul are situated at a different level; and part of myself, in a sense, is no concern of anyone but God.

In the old days – I wonder why I am speaking in the past – parents used to teach their very young children to live 'under the all-seeing eye of God', who could see whatever they did even secretly, and who knew all the thoughts of their hearts. And so we learned that we were not free to act exactly as we pleased, but as God expected us to act. So conscience developed, to play its part in unifying our lives: since what was most secret in us ought not to be at odds with our outward way of being or behaving. Otherwise we felt deceitful, by consenting to appear or behave without regard to what we might be thinking inside. This training in the sense of the presence of God 'who sounds the heart and reins' is very much at a discount today as a limitation placed on 'freedom of conscience'. 'Conscience', you see, has changed its meaning!

I remember paying a visit a few years ago to a poor church built by native Christians in a village in the forests of Cameroon. A thatched roof and wooden frame were sup-

ported by pairs of cylindrical pillars of whitewashed earth.
When you went in, you were immediately struck by the sight
of two enormous eyes crudely painted on the first two pillars.
A pair of eyes adorned the next pillars further in, and so on.
Thus, these simple folk tried to emphasise the presence of
All-seeing, All-hearing God. So, our religious concept of man
sees him as a being whose entire outward behaviour should
reflect what he is in his heart, under the eye of God. Whereas
the behaviour of present-day man tends rather to be governed
by social and political considerations and the ideal of being 'a
man for all seasons'. For communism, a training in one's duty
to society and an attitude of submissiveness to the collective
good are essential. Without denying the value of this sort of
training, we have to recognise the limitations of such a moral
system, since it leaves domestic behaviour untouched, and
even more so, the individual's inner life: I mean his motives
and emotions. Anything goes, so long as it does not impinge
on the rights of others. This is the kind of morality now gain-
ing ground, and it would be a mistake to imagine that we can
completely escape the influence of the environment in this
respect.

When, in fervour of heart, you come to the Fraternity to give
your lives to Christ, you do this in all generosity of spirit: also,
because you really want to love God more than anything else,
and your fellow-men to the exclusion of yourselves. And so I
shall ask you this: Are you capable of doing it? Now, of course
none of us is capable of doing this straightaway and so we
have to work at it, at becoming free and freer to love without
reserve. This is an indispensable preparatory stage which people sometimes evade, either because they are deluded, or
because they are inexperienced, or because they too readily
believe that good intentions are enough, especially where loving is concerned. It comes as a shock to them to discover that
love, by its own power, is not automatically able to achieve
what it naturally aspires to do. We are not able to make our
love instantly effective. But it is within our power, by effort, to
make ourselves able. And this, surely, is the point of God's
commandments and the aim of the Gospel's moral precepts –
to show us the ways to be followed in learning how to love.

The first thing we have to do is to know ourselves for the
persons we are and as the world in which we are living makes

us. Next, we must learn to know ourselves in what differen-
tiates us from other people and this is not easy: we are easily
put off and discouraged by the various forms of weakness,
deceitfulness and selfishness which we discover to be ours: we
are not the men we thought ourselves to be. Lastly, we have to
decide what sort of self-discipline we need.

Here I should like to quote you something written by Père
Besnard,[25] illustrating this need by an arresting simile:

'We are like a little city in miniature. The ancients used
to say that man is a little world in miniature, a microcosm;
we might say micropolis. We are a little town. Like most of
our modern towns, each of us has developed in a haphazard
way: a new road here, a building run up there, a block of
flats pulled down further on. Similarly, in our own lives, we
get to know people and things in all sorts of different ways,
we run into new faces, we suffer ordeals, we endure bom-
bardments; earthquakes and landslides occur; we rebuild,
we patch up old buildings: I mean the riven structure of our
psyche. Then again, the town is one where the different dis-
tricts are often in conflict, conscious or unconscious,
declared or underground. These are our internal tensions,
our unresolved contradictions, our micro- or
macro-neuroses. And all this notwithstanding, the city, this
micropolis, is supposed to become the micro-Kingdom of
God. Just as today in the cities where we live, we need firm,
wise and practical local government, so too we ourselves
need firm, wise and practical policies if we are to become
what we want to be. That is what self-discipline is.'

For the person who believes in God and in God's adoption
of man in Christ our brother, freedom does not consist is doing
what we want, but in wanting to be ready to do what God
wants us to do. You will tell me that this is very obvious. But
in fact we are always forgetting how obvious this is, since
man's will and God's will do not always coincide. To act in accordance with obligations embodying what God wants us to
do is not within the compass of facile spontaneity!

Obeying God, as I see it, takes place on two levels. First of all
there is that fundamental obedience to the Divine Law as laid

down in the Ten Commandments, and binding on everyone. But in our own journeying towards God, we go farther than this. By offering ourselves to Christ, we choose a vocation, a mission, with obligations of its own. And this gives rise to very special obligations for each of us – personalised obligations, I might say. Here again, you will tell me that this is obvious. You have thought carefully about what a vocation to be a Little Brother of the Gospel implies, you have chosen this vocation, you understand what its obligations are. You will, I dare say, have already realised that you won't succeed in carrying them out. To imagine or say otherwise would mean you still had illusions about yourself.

It is not in fact enough that our intentions and desires – St Paul goes so far as to say his deliberate decisions – should conform to God's demands. In our nice, open-hearted but illusion-ridden spontaneity, we do conform to the image which God gives us of ourselves. But when it comes to putting things into practice, we cannot do it. There is nothing new in this. The Apostle Paul experienced the same problem, which was all the more painful for him since he had met Christ. '*I cannot understand my own behaviour: I fail to carry out the things I want to do, and I find myself doing the very things I hate*'.[26]

That is the way we are; that is why we need a rule and system of freely accepted constraints, for these alone can enable us to govern our lives and learn to love properly. We think we are free, but we are not. Christ's absolute freedom could not induce him to will what was wrong. But we are quite capable of willing it, or more accurately of giving ourselves over to it. But what then do we mean when we say that freedom for us is associated with the possibility of choosing what is wrong? If we were indeed to choose this, wouldn't it prove that we were free? That depends on what we mean by freedom. Sometimes we define it just so, as the ability to choose anything, to will anything. If that were true, we should have to say that Christ was the least free of all men, since he could not choose what was wrong. Some people even do wrong to assert their freedom, to prove to themselves how free they are! Christ always spontaneously chose the best. Isn't freedom precisely this living spontaneity, intimately linked to the dynamics of divine and human life, alone capable of bringing a spiritual being to the fulness of love? For this freedom to act untrammelled, it must be enlightened by a very pure awareness and vision of the good which prevents spontaneity from turning to evil under the appearance of good. Is it in any case possible for a man really to desire what is wrong? Absolute evil is not to be encountered in human life, since man always sees evil in terms of a good to be desired and capable of yielding an immediate satisfaction. There is an appearance of good, a partial good for us. This is why sinful man's state of soul is so complex. In any case, he is not completely free, since enslaved and limited by many factors. And the question then is to know what to do about making ourselves free. For this becomes the more attainable, the more clearly we evaluate things and divest ourselves of mirages and illusions. We shall then be in a better situation to destroy the enslaving factors to which our inner freedom is subjected.

Our first effort therefore must be to train our conscience. The value-judgments that we have to pass on our plans, our actions and attitudes of mind must be more enlightened. A great nearness to God, which is bestowed on us in prayer and contemplation, contributes to the refining of our awarness by the new light it throws on people and events. We then have to concentrate on strengthening the spiritual will as something distinct from those instinctive attractions and impulses prompting us towards things which give us an immediate satisfaction or a more or less selfish, emotional or carnal pleasure. Enlightened by the Spirit of Truth, our conscience will teach us to know what is best and our will will then be able to desire it. Such inner freedom is not easily achieved. It postulates that we make a habit of obeying God, which is the same as learning to control ourselves in conformity to God's law and the Gospel law. Self-control means consenting to restrain oneself, to force oneself to do what one would not do spontaneously. So we must not confuse freedom with this kind of spontaneity, this being in fact blind impulse, instinct, ungoverned emotion. This is only apparent spontaneity. People talk a lot about spontaneity without considering that the word conceals an ambiguity. True spontaneity is something quite different, since that wells up from an enlightened heart. And this is not to be confused with what is called spontaneity, prompting us to do what gives immediate satisfaction. Consequently we often find ourselves faced with having to make a painful choice. Owing to weakness, to illusion or to not knowing how far such and such an impulsive choice will lead us, we end up in sorry situations. Sometimes we genuinely do not know what the consequences of our actions will be. Take the case, for instance, of a household where husband and wife really love each other. Irresponsibly, frivolously, rashly, one of the partners suddenly falls in love with someone else. What is to be done? To follow where this spontaneous passion leads would be some people's solution – as being the only way of being true to oneself. According to this school of thought, it is right to act on the impulse of the moment, hence on the spontaneity of passion, even if the choice so made is not the one which would be made in the cold light of reason. There are, admittedly, situations where we are faced with painful, tragic choice. We have to be convinced that obeying Christ is a course inevitably leading to the Cross: the way of suffering, I mean, not only of suffering to which we assent or submit, but also of suffering which we shall not hesitate to impose on ourselves, so that we can always be free to choose the best.

The Gospel states this clearly, but we are very naturally prone to forget the passages in which Christ speaks about renunciation: *'Deny yourself'* . . . *'If you do not deny yourself, you cannot be my disciple'* . . . *'He who loses his own life will find it'* . . . *'If your eye offends you, pull it out'*. . . . And we can be sure that Christ will not ask us to renounce our essential selves, or what is best, or what makes us men and disciples of his. We must deny ourselves at a different level from that. Love consists in being centred on God and on our fellow-men. We have to renounce being centred on ourselves. Loving is not to be done as the moment may prompt. Christ is not inviting us to an indiscriminate sort of loving. How ambiguous the word love is too – how loaded with contradictions – like man himself!

So, ought we to impose – I really mean impose – a personal rule of conduct on ourselves and compel ourselves to observe it? Should we voluntarily take measures to check and so correct those tendencies, habits and inclinations which prevent us from being the men, the Christians, the religious, that we ought to be? Constraints imposed from outside are odious and harmful. Those which we ourselves freely impose are creative and beneficial.

That is the problem. To which some people might reply that all this is naturally achieved by the constraints of daily life and work, without our needing to impose further constraints of our own. But we are bound to admit that these natural constraints are not sufficient. And this is why the problem of self-discipline arises, and the need for a rule, and for a personal rule of life.

Obviously there is nothing to be gained by scorning the ordinary necessities of life, since these are essential to physical and mental health. No one can forgo regular meals, sleep, recreation and rest, without asking for trouble. This goes without saying and we would not dispute it. People do however forget that we also have similar needs at the emotional and spiritual level too, and these cannot be ignored with impunity either. The spiritual life cannot be led in disregard of certain fundamental needs.

The Fathers of the Church, the Early Fathers, used to speak of the *psychic* as contrasted with the *spiritual* man. Even if their language was influenced by the philosophy of their own day, the insight which it expressed serves us still. The psychic being is man taken at the level of those perceptions and feelings which come within the province of psychology: the zone in which sense-evidence is paramount. But, if the influence of sense-evidence is too strong, there is the risk that a man will become trapped in self-absorbtion at the level of the senses. The psychic man, according to the Fathers, is an imperfect man. The spiritual man, by way of contrast, is the Christ-like man, the man who has discovered his spiritual stature, who has consented to rise and grow beyond the psychic state, his spirit made vigorous by the seed of eternal life which he bears within him. We do not reach this stage overnight. Our spiritual growth will consist in frequenting God's presence, in absorbing the wisdom of the Gospel, in learning to love our fellow-men so disinterestedly and clear-sightedly as to make it possible for them to become spiritual beings too.

So, the mere fact of joining the Fraternity and of fully accepting its vocation is not enough in itself. We are not what we ought to be and if ever at any moment in our lives we stop trying to become the spiritual man which we have not yet become, by this very fact we shall also stop living up to our vocation. For the choice once made has to go on being made. And in any case we have this obligation to keep growing, incumbent on man whatever his sphere of life. A man who believes himself to be a doctor because he has passed his medical exams is mistaken: for, if he is aware of his responsibilities, he will have to start and go on becoming a doctor by practising. He will have to keep himself up to date, will have to specialise, read specialist publications and allow himself enough time for doing this – or risk not being what he ought to be.

All too often, religious imagine that it is easy to be a religious. Just as the needs of life, especially of psychic life, have to be met, so too the spiritual life has its needs, and these are harder to accept and sort out. We have already talked about what I called the elements of contemplative life and of your religious life. These are just as important to the spiritual life as meals, sleep, work, human relationships and recreation are to the psychic life. We have to realise this. We not only have a relationship with God and a relationship with our fellow-men; we also have a relationship with ourselves – as we have already said.

I shall now offer you a few observations on present-day attitudes of mind, with the good points and problems that go with them. Why in modern Christian and religious life has there been an almost complete abandoning of the idea of self-discipline, of regularity and even of rule? Regularity consists in observing a rule of life in the deeper sense of the words, not in the sense of observing regulations or a time-table. We may for a start say that our world is full of contradictions. On the one hand we see that mankind has seldom been subjected to so many regulations impinging on every sphere of life. Be it in his political life, his social life, his professional life, he is everywhere obliged to conform to very strict codes of conduct. And these codes tend to become stricter and stricter, the farther he advances in a progressively more specialised world. Being forced to submit to a specialised discipline however, he loses a wider appreciation of the world at large: hence perhaps the concommittant reaction, in the spiritual sphere, of rejecting all rule and all authority. These are sometimes rejected root and branch; people strive to be free of them because they are thirsty for freedom, for personal responsibility and for genuine spontaneity.

It must be admitted that here we find ourselves in a difficult predicament since this contempt for regulations and formalities is often not concerned with matters of vital importance. Abuse of authority in religious life, an authority based on a narrow conception of religious perfection which no longer corresponds to the basic requirements of an obedience due to Christ and to a vocation emanating from him, can produce, by way of reaction, an attitude of generalised rejection.

Here then is our first problem – a psychological one. But there is another, arising from the primacy accorded to personal experience as against the traditional consensus of other people's experience as regards the obligations of the spiritual life and even on occasion of morality. True, in certain matters nothing can take the place of personal experience. Even so, this experience must be informed by an ideal, by a goal to be attained. No one can claim the right to experience everything. Must one have experienced evil, so as to know what it is? Some people may think so. Must one have experienced the various stages of human life, purely for information, before consecrating one's body to chastity? Must one have experienced the gamut of moral disorders before being able to help other people in the same plight? The question is even put: are priests, having taken a vow of celibacy, really competent to help married people – as priests having had no experience of married life. But is this really the sort of experience we expect of men responsible for passing on the Gospel Law and the demands of Christ?

Then again, you are aware of the confusion now reigning over the way to bring up the young, a confusion which affects family, school and university. This same confusion obtains over the sort of training that priests and religious should get in novitiates and seminaries. Is training even possible in present conditions? And if so, what form should it take?

Too often the trainees are now allowed to conduct their own experiments. And here, I suppose, we see a reaction against the indisputably bad effects of a theory of training which paid little regard to personal freedom and responsibility. We cannot turn our backs on this problem. We shall have to try and find a solution for it, on the basis of a balanced evaluation of the Gospel's requirements, seen altogether as a law of love – yes, certainly, but not as a law of an indiscriminate loving! For what we are called to involves our travelling by way of the Cross and can only be achieved at the price of certain forms of renunciation. For Christ was not content to say, '*Love one another as I have loved you.*' He showed us the way to freedom, which lies by way of struggling against our secret servitude to sin, to our weaknesses and to our bad habits.

The modern generation attaches more importance to what it calls spontaneity than to disciplined behaviour. Hence, you may even hear religious say that it is more perfect to make a spontaneous act of poverty or obedience than to take a vow, which transforms spontaneity into obligation. Rejection of disciplined behaviour or of self-imposed obligation comes from thinking that by not being bound by a promise there will be greater spontaneity of love. To which I reply that it is precisely because of my loving spontaneity that I want to bind myself and thus increase my likelihood of being faithful. It would be self-deception to imagine oneself as spontaneously capable of loving in the purest, most disinterested way, without assuming any obligations at the same time. Hence the lack of enthusiasm for a rule of life.

There is also an observable tendency to play down the concept of obligation, on the pretext that it curtails our freedom. This problem, closely related to the previous one, involves disputing the value of giving an undertaking to anyone else, even to God. Promising to do something or to behave in a certain way is basically unimportant: the important thing is to do it! Well, yes. But the sentiment does not tally with the facts. At the root of it is a deliberate rejection of all constraint, even moral. Our contemporaries have what amounts to a congenital distaste for all constraint, since modern life imposes so many constraints on them. Urban life and most forms of technical work involve a veritable mesh of every kind of constraint. No one is free of it. The other day I was looking in a shop window and saw a pottery ashtray covered in writing. In the centre were the words, 'To hell with them all!' The constraining factors were inscribed all round this: red traffic-lights, the underground, work, public transport, noisy neighbours, traffic jams, no-parking signs. Nerves are on edge, people are fed up. Under these constraints, people imagine that at least when following Christ in the religious life they will be able to escape from all constraint and be free at last! People erect a somewhat simplistic picture for themselves: living like St Francis of Assisi, the Little Poor-man, singing the Lord's praises in natural freedom. And they forget about those freedom-conferring constraints which he imposed on himself with such remorseless vigour. These were, you may be sure, of a very different order from the outward ones affecting us at the psychological level, destructive ones, causing neuroses which incapacitate us for true freedom!

To all this we must add a subtle change in the attitude to sin, since attention is now largely concentrated on social sin, on the sin of injustice, on what harms others, in consequence of which people are hardly aware of inward sin, of sins of intention, of sins of thought or imagination, to which God alone is privy. Do people understand what we mean when we talk of inner purity? Anyone can see how lightheartedly not only the laity but religious too read books and go to shows inevitably involving inner temptation and even transgression. People seem to think this unimportant!

And indeed there is a point of view according to which there is no such thing as a moral code anymore, with a result that one hardly dares to mention it.

To see how true this is, you have only to consider how outraged public opinion becomes and how the press reacts over subjects like contraception, abortion, euthansia and suicide. It is now even maintained that these matters do not come within the scope of morality. It is the same thing with problems of sexuality, more and more, it would seem, to be exclusively regarded as biological phenomena.

The only laws people recognise today are scientific ones. The result is that man comes to be treated as an object like any other in the complex order of creation. Man's private and social life seems more and more subordinated to the dictates of economics, sociology, depth-psychology and sexual biology. How then can one talk about a moral law which has its basis in the divine destiny of man? And even chastity in the religious and priestly life is primarily regarded from the psychological or sexual angle. We must certainly agree on what we mean by sexuality. For people say very little about affection, self-giving, love and friendship, while having a great deal to say about sex education for adolescents, for children and for married couples, as also about a balanced sex-life for the celibate. This particular aspect of sexuality is no longer linked to a training in love, tenderness and affection or the deeper spiritual aspirations which nonetheless flourish in human love, even if now being ignored. Man is as it were being fragmented. Sexuality is, to be sure, what distinguishes a man from a woman, influencing each at every stage of life. It influences their outlook, the kinds of activity they pursue, their aptitudes, their feelings and, above all, their emotional life — even at the most exalted level, be it said. The Virgin Mary was a woman in the full sense of the word, just as Jesus was a complete man and truly man.

You can never define the core of man, the seat of consciousness and personality. You may analyse the various zones of his nature, from his psychological make-up to his physiological reflexes; you may study the way he expresses himself and the way he behaves as social being; and from this you may deduce a series of laws to help you work out what he needs and how best to train and develop his faculties. But even doing this, you miss the essential, while man has lost his sense of identity meanwhile.

I remember having seen a television discussion on the nature of man; those taking part were a language specialist, a psychologist and a biologist. Though really serious scientists, they admitted themselves at a loss, even after synthesising all the scientific data now available, to define the nature of man, and concluded that any such definition would always have to be made in terms of philosophy or religion. Owing to the very complexity of the problems arising today, we cannot but resort to these sciences, but we must always remember the limited scope of each. That is why it is no use envisaging a reformation of religious life exclusively in terms of group-psychology, or questioning for historical reasons or out of respect for some new exegetical trends the fundamental elements of religious life as lived within the Church throughout the ages and validated by Christian experience. Yes, of course there have been abuses, there are things now that need to be corrected, and in doing this it is right to take account of psychology or of a healthy notion of freedom. But the religious will not regard it as his job to be a professional psychologist; his experience has to be of the paths of prayer.

Another problem arises from the fact that many young people have a spontaneous feeling of *invulnerability* and imagine that they can get away with anything, provided that they have the right intentions. To imagine that you can see everything, keep any company, take every kind of risk, and yet remain unscathed is a mistake likely to bring harmful results and to leave lasting traces. The married man concerned about his family and the man who has embraced the religous life must alike stay aware of their frailty in the pursuit of Christian holiness, in their faithfulness to Christian chastity, as also in the performance of their spiritual mission and in perseverance in a life of prayer. I do not say that it may not sometimes be necessary to take risks; but these must be calculated ones with a view to procuring a greater good, taken in lucid awareness of our own fraility. Far from being invulnerable, we are infinitely frail: and religious life and works of the Spirit are particularly so. As the Apostle Paul says, we possess a treasure in an earthenware pot. our vocation is a highly spiritual treasure and we ourselves are very fragile vessels. When the discharging of our evangelistic mission requires us to live in certain environments – where prostitution, for instance, or drug-taking are rife – we must be clear in our minds that these environments will exert a progressive influence on our souls, even though we may not notice this. All the more reason for being aware of our frailty and remembering the treasure for which we are responsible and the people whom, as disciples of the Lord, we have to be.

The present generation is characterised by another attitude: a *horror of artificiality,* of formalism, and a deep need for the genuine. Naturally, whatever is artificial is to be eschewed. The formalism arising from it is an evil, a paralysis, clear evidence of a lack of authenticity. So we have to know what is artificial and what is not. For instance, is it formalism to impose a rule of life on yourself? I should say, it depends what rule you mean. If you mean a living rule, one intended to help you renounce yourself and enable you to love God and man as our vocation requires, then that cannot be described as artificial. The same holds good when discussing the environment. For instance, the modern urban environment is artificial, in the original sense of the word; it has been contrived by human art. Man has conceived and built the town and, if his sole consideration has been to do this as cheaply and easily as possible, it is not particularly surprising that an inhuman environment is the result: an artificial one in the true meaning of the word. And this is an evil which must surely be opposed and rejected.

In this case, might we not say that the cloistered life of monks and nuns is artificial. To this, we may glibly reply that it certainly is, since it is not a normal way of life but the product of a gamut of rules which, like that of enclosure, are artificial! And, of course, if the invisible world did not exist, this way of life would indeed be artificial, since not geared to the facts of life. Contrariwise, the environment of genuine cloistered life – I am not talking here about the times when things go wrong – with its isolation from the hurly-burly of the world, its separateness from society, its silence, its consecration to prayer, contemplation and study, is not artificial in the least, if it is ordered in terms of the interior relationships of individual and community with God and in terms of a contemplative mission in the Church. A life entirely centred on that very real world of the angels, the saints, the Trinity, Christ and the Virgin, is not an artificial life but the very reverse: a life unfolding in a deeply authentic environment.

In all the different attitudes of which we have spoken, there is, we have seen, an element of truth, but also too absolute a rejection of things of value. The same thing may be said about some people's view of the traditional conception of the novitiate. It is artificial, they say. What is so artificial about the novitiate? If you want to train young people for living in communion with the invisible, if you want to create a habit of union with God, to make the conscience responsive to the laws of God and Gospel and to establish perseverance in prayer, you have to spend some time at least in an environment favourable to this type of life.

You cannot do everything at once. To imagine yourself instantly able to live immersed in the world and available to your fellow-men and at the same time entirely devoted to the things of God, is to harbour more illusions than one! The Christian bearer of what Christ has revealed about the Father and about our relationship with him, is a man straddled between two worlds, even though called to live his vocation in a completely unified, normal human life. Christ was a perfectly unified man, although obliged in a certain sense to divide his life between God his Father and man his brother. Saying this, I know it does not apply entirely in Christ's case. All the same, his agony and painful obedience in Gethsemane revealed a for us unimaginable tension between divine nature and human nature, between infinite and finite, between eternal and temporal, between death and life. In Christ, we see, in supreme and absolute degree, that mysterious living reality which we too have within us: the imprinted image of God himself, henceforth making us creatures destined for eternal life. So do not let us speak lightly of the demands which this seed of eternity obtrudes on Christian and religious life. Because of it, many Christians at present feel a deep need to withdraw from the world, to find solitude and peace; and this is the spontaneous reaction of a healthy spiritual life.

I should also like to draw attention to another aspect of contemporary Christian and religious thought: I mean *the cult of human values.* So it is that some religious feel impelled, by way of reaction to the notion of separateness from the world, to re-introduce human values into their religious life, without always being aware how misleading and unrealistic it is to do this. Christ never despised true human values and I am certainly not advocating that we as religious should despise them either. But your consecration to Christ and participation in his mission oblige you to make a choice. You cannot do everything. And a man can only have one ruling passion in his life. If I make Christ's design, his wishes, his reason for living, mine I ought to be passionately absorbed in his apostolic mission. I am not capable of simultaneously embracing all human values and of devoting myself to the absorbing activities which they invite as well.

Christ clearly demanded of his disciples not the despising but the complete rejection of the entire range of human values. For renunciation of sin is not the only renunciation required of those who are called to enter the religious life. When Christ invited the rich young man to sell all his possessions and to leave his family and follow him, he was in fact demanding the renunciation of the best of human values. It was the same when Christ told his apostles to leave their nets and give up their jobs. These human values have to be abandoned. So we have to know what we are trying to do. It is no use clinging to illusions. God knows how alluring the world is and what a variety of tasks and delights it has to offer. But the ill-mastered need to see everything and to know everything can lead to terrible disorders. Must we, to meet the world on an equal footing, meet all men on their own ground, experience everything for ourselves? Because conversation happens to turn to a television programme or a football match, must I suppose my duty lies in spending my evenings glued to my set and my week-ends watching sporting events? What would become of me? For I should also have to see all the week's new films. Surely the same problem must arise for professional people and politicians too?

I have met religious who, their General Chapter having laid stress on respect for human values, have asked their Superior for permission to go to the theatre, to concerts or to the ballet. I took the liberty of asking them how they found time for doing this and what was left of the specific quality of their consecrated life. If you no longer devote enough time to meditating on Scripture, to studying theology, to praying, to being permeated by God to the point where you can communicate him to others, who is going to do it instead?

I used to know a married man, a father of three, a doctor; his wife was a marriage counsellor. He was completely devoted to the people of his district, available to treat them night and day. I can tell you, neither husband nor wife had time to watch television, listen to the radio or go to the cinema! They had one sole care: to be faithful to their vocations as doctor and marriage counsellor. Should the life of a religious be less exacting?

It sometimes happens that you find a more balanced approach and more authentic devotion to a task among laymen than you do among religious. Isn't this perhaps because the latter, on the pretext that their vocation demands it of them, try to experience every aspect of human life? Certainly, we ought to be ready to cope with any aspect of life. This is what makes the problems of apostolic life so complex. But it is still always true that prolonged prayer must play an important part in our lives if we want these to stay effectively consecrated to our essential task and mission. We cannot allow our way of life to make us less capable of fulfilling our task; and the task will always require self-discipline and renunciation. We cannot do whatever we fancy; we have to behave in a way consonant with the needs of our particular vocation.

Nor should we overlook another aspect of contemporary society: *distraction.* This can reach such a point that many young people become seriously unbalanced. There are too many centres of interest. You have to know how to control yourself, if your powers of concentration are not to be undermined: the morning and evening papers, the wireless, the television, world events, industrial action, political crises, housing, the family, balancing the budget – that's enough to go on with! All this is the inevitable product of the way the modern world is organised, as well of the greater opportunities for leisure and of the greater number of places of interest and entertainment that we can reach. In so far as your mission obliges you to stay living among men in the world, you are being influenced by the environment, and the resulting distraction is the very opposite of that deep spirit of attention proper to the things of God. For the union of the spirit with God engenders unity and simplification of inner perception, and this becomes wisdom because it scrutinises all from above, as though from the stand-point of the Creator. We have to master the multiple. You will soon find this to be so if you are faithful to prayer. When you are alone for days on end with God, you know from your own experience that you then acquire some degree of inner simplicity. Your vision of things changes, since it becomes the reflection of Christ's own vision of the whole creation and in particular of the hearts of men – his Kingdom. The misuse of audio-visual techniques can run counter to this inner simplification. A too exclusive reliance on these methods in religious instruction can lead to a diffuse and superficial quality of faith. For the appeal is no longer directed to the spirit, but to the senses, and it is all too easy to forget that for man the latter should be the gates of the soul.

We ought to be all the more on our guard against these

risks, given the impossibility of escaping the effects of audio-visual technology, and we cannot in fact refuse to use these techniques, given the place they have now come to occupy in our society. One whole dimension of man, his inner dimension, risks being paralysed by them, and this leads to the atrophy of spiritual intuition, which is itself the basis for contemplation of the things of God. Should a contemplative religious give up using these techniques? Well, certainly he should go beyond them. What St John of the Cross had to say about purging the imagination in prayer is still valid for our own day, for this touches the very nature of things.

We must also say a word about *Christian asceticism.* Here a general confusion reigns. It sometimes happens that we miss one truth by applying its name to something else. The word asceticism has long been applied to an asceticism typically monastic. Asceticism, people used to say, is what monks have to practise. Today, many Christians are themselves discovering that they too need to practise a form of asceticism adapted to their lives in the world. But they are uncertain what to do, since up to the present the forms of asceticism available to them have only been those more or less appropriate to monastic life: that is to say, penance, living by a rule, silence and maybe fasting, abstinence and vigils. Asceticism was more or less confined to these activities. Now, it is important not to confuse penance with asceticism, since these are two different things. I have often heard laymen, and religious too for that matter, say we no longer need to practise asceticism, that is to say, '*exercises*', because life itself will take care of that! – thus replacing the traditional concept of voluntary, with what they term '*circumstantial*' asceticism. Consequently we shall have to consider what the aim and true nature of asceticism should be.

People point out, doubtless rightly, that opportunities for devotion and self-denial keep occurring in daily life. Now, the duties of our state in life, the faithful discharging of duties to the family, the harsh daily discipline imposed by working conditions, transport, getting up early, are all forms of exacting constraint. But do they amount to asceticism? I must say, I really don't know: for this depends on the way we accept these constraints, which may in themselves have the very opposite effect and produce serious character-disorders. The constraints of life ought, they say, to rouse inner reactions which of themselves should enable us to master those same constraints and use them so to discipline ourselves as to be more available to love and serve other people better. Unfortunately, the constraints arising from our environment can produce the very opposite results. A man and wife, for instance, whole-heartedly engaged in apostolic work or political activities, may find themselves living in conditions no longer permitting marital intimacy and thus leading to the gradual breakdown of their marriage. Can you honestly say that that sort of life qualifies as ascetic? There is muddled thinking here. The constraints of modern life are extraneous to us. They are difficult conditions which may indeed offer opportunities for devotion and self-denial, but asceticism is an internal constraint which we voluntarily impose on ourselves, so that we can turn the extraneous demands of life to greater good, not let them be the means of our own destruction. No one can do without an apprenticeship in self-discipline freely imposed from within. Words must not be allowed to confuse the issue.

In conclusion, we may say that asceticism consists in learning, by voluntarily imposing constraints on ourselves, to master events and the emotions that these arouse in us. These constraints, whether freely imposed or accepted, are either very private ones or those embodied in a rule, which in any case must be adapted to the individual. I speak of constraint, hence of renunciation; for constraint implies renunciation, even of things in themselves good but which in certain cases become obstacles to the achieving of a greater good. He who renounces marriage, renounces something good. By the same token, a certain degree of wealth puts very valuable assets within one's reach, I mean cultural assets. The passion of love, the need for beauty, cannot always be satisfied, for renunciation imposes a series of choices, fitting us to choose the better of two courses as individual vocation and inner purity may require. In olden days, people used to speak of the need for cleanliness of spirit, of cleanliness of the senses, of the imagination and of the heart. The expression was related to the function that asceticism was intended to perform. Going to some kinds of

show or reading some kinds of book, is bound to leave its mark
on us. It is not within our power to prevent the cumulative
effects of these activities in the long run from undermining our
proper inner reactions, our spiritual energy and our strength
of will. Thus our inner resistance is weakened, and one day
this will show on the outside. I say outside, since the tendency
today is to judge infidelity only in terms of outward behaviour.
People are in agreement, tacitly at least, that the vow of
chastity in the celibate life means renouncing marriage and
avoiding falling in love. But a little flirting, a certain amount of
broadmindedness, not having scruples about going to films or
shows which stimulate sexual desire and titillate the imagination – this is not regarded as being unfaithful to our vow, all
the while it does not cause us to renounce the celibate life.
Aren't we forgetting that what we have given Christ is not
merely the state of celibacy but our very hearts and souls? As
with marriage, so with celibacy: Christ does not ask for a
merely external loyalty, but loyalty of heart and soul. Christ
has made this very clear.[27]   Now, this kind of loyalty is not
possible without asceticism, consisting in rejecting not merely
sin, but even things excellent in themselves, or activities of
their nature good but tending to diminish or spoil our aptitude
for chastity, for prayer, for universal love, in a words, for
Christian perfection and carrying out our mission, and so
diminishing what we ought to be in the eyes of God and men.
So, you will say, what is to be done? I cannot tell you here
what a healthy asceticism would require of each of you.
Nothing can take the place of your own judgment and personal efforts in finding out how you ought to behave. Take the
Gospel's insistence on renunciation seriously. Adopt a bit of
psychology and make no doubts about your vulnerability. Pay
attention to the inner purity of your intentions. People don't
think enough about this.

Learn too and above all to know yourself. You remember
how, at the beginning of this talk, I quoted the simile of the
city built as circumstance dictated, without planning. Be
aware of the degree to which you are in control of yourself.
Sometimes you will find that, as a method of self-government,
diplomacy works better than constraint. You will need advice,
you will need help. Ruling yourself is not as easy as you may
suppose. We have to listen to our brothers' advice and open

our hearts to them: for no two cases are ever alike. Our individual difficulties are not apparent. Our brothers do not always recognise them, since their difficulties are different from ours. The quest for self-knowledge should not however be allowed to lead to introspection, for this too is distraction and drives us in on ourselves. Let us stay simple and open. Though self-knowledge is essential to self-government, we must avoid all self-centredness. We have to accept being what we are, for this is what we shall remain until our dying day, despite our efforts and the little progress we make. Your character-defects, the traces left on you by your past history, a certain degree of emotional inconstancy: these are constituent parts of your personality and will hardly alter. You have to realise this, if you want to rule yourself without self-deception.

Self-knowledge cannot be a source of deep peace unless achieved in that divine light which is the source of that same knowledge. As St John of the Cross says, experience of God gives us an understanding of our state as creatures, of our condition as sinners. Let us hold on to this vision, and so be modest, humble, prudent, aware of our frailty but at peace, since this we cannot change: and hence content to be loved for what we are by our Creator and Father.

As the consequence of this self-knowledge, we learn to conquer ourselves and control ourselves at three different levels. At the first, we have to forbid ourselves whatever conduces to sin. This ought to be clear to everyone. Even so, a certain feeling of invulnerability often encourages us to brave situations which ordinarily lead to sin, to inward sin at least. Avoiding any such situation is part of asceticism. And if we do decide to run risks, we must always do this from the highest motives of charity and apostolic service. Here above all is where we need our brothers' advice in making a proper appreciation of the situation.

The second level is that of the obligations of your vocation. These are expressed in a rule, not merely defining your vocation and mission but describing the principal means to be used in accomplishing it. We shall certainly have to examine ourselves on this score. You are all aware of the need for a rule of life: it would be folly to imagine that we could do without a rule. Yet a rule in itself is not sufficient.

The third level is the one on which we shall have to expend our efforts: that of personalising the rule, that is to say, of applying the rule to our individual case. Here too you will need help and advice from your brothers, and particularly from your superiors. For it is your superiors' mission to help you when you find difficulty in translating the stipulations of the rule into practical terms to meet your particular needs and circumstances. You have to learn how to impose a personal rule on yourself. The single rule needed by any community is diversified in the lives of the individual members. And it is precisely the function of superiors to make the rule a living one by adapting it to each fraternity and each member as need and circumstance dictate.

We must not let things get too complicated. The further we progress along the spiritual way, the simpler ought the rule we need to be. Need for a rule differs therefore at successive stages of our life. In Brother Charles's last year at Tammanrasset, he did not feel the same need for a rule as when he had been living at Beni Abbes. This was due to a simplification, to a transformation, not to a degeneration, of his devotion.

But this is not always the case, and so we ought to be careful over our motives as regards our need for a rule of life. Even so, it would still be a mistake to try and make the same rule of life apply at every stage of spiritual life. In fact I don't think that could be done without relapsing into formal observance. Fidelity to the practical demands of a vocation is something very much alive, constantly changing, always needing to be re-thought in terms of the actual situation, of our progress and of our personal and spiritual maturity. How to be faithful to a rule of life is therefore a question we have to keep asking ourselves anew, since no one can be either a Christian or a religious merely by good-will: this is something we have to keep striving to become.

VI

A Church of Sinners: Stumbling Block or Rock of Faith?

By faith and by belonging to Christ we are consecrated and brought into relationship with the Church. As brothers of Jesus and sons of God, we are also sons of the Church, generated by her in baptism. In her, we repent of our sins; she is the keeper of our Christian conscience. How is it then that, although we can easily accept the Gospel and come very close to the heart of it in meditation, we find our life in the Church so beset with problems? As we cannot belong to Christ without belonging to the Church, there is a very real problem here, with which we shall have to come to grips.

When Jesus, having gathered his first apostles round him, saw the time approaching when he would end his earthly span by dying and being glorified, he could not leave his disciples and the generations to come deprived entirely of his presence. This was when he conceived the Church and brought it into existence. I need not remind you of the words and deeds by which Christ laid down the foundations and essential structure of this first community.

When we read St Paul's epistles, we cannot help being struck by the Apostle's determination faithfully to preserve what he had himself received from the Lord, *'The fact is, brothers, and I want you to realise this: the Good News I have been preaching is not a human message, not something I was given by men, but something I learned through a revelation from Jesus Christ*[28] *... If anyone preaches a version of the Good News different from the one we have already preached to you, whether it be ourselves or an angel from heaven, he is to be condemned.*[29]

Yes, the founding of this Church, as established by Christ and as seen by us today, is the sole guarantor of the Gospel. Not but what the Church has been challenged and its function denied, even though all the other Churches, including those most hostile to episcopal church-order, accept the authority of those scriptural passages which speak of its foundation. They interpret them differently, however.

Having led Simon to confess his faith, Jesus gave him a new name: Peter. It was the first time anyone had been called this. No one had ever been called 'Stone' or 'Rock' before. *'So now I say to you: You are Peter and on this Rock I shall build my Church, and the Gates of Hell will not prevail against her.*[31]   The imagery in Christ's words clearly reflects the concept of building up an organised society, a people united and ready for the struggle to come. This people would have to endure the onslaughts of the Gates of Hell, that is to say, of the powers of evil, but these would not prevail. And then Jesus added, *'Simon, Simon! Satan, you must know, has got his wish to sift you all like wheat; but I have prayed for you, Simon, that your faith may not fail, and once you have recovered, you in your turn must strengthen your brothers.*[31]   Some people maintain that he only meant a privileged position for Simon in relation to his immediate companions. But in the light of what happened immediately after the Ascension, it is hard to imagine that Christ was not thinking of the Church itself. I do not intend discussing every aspect of the Church with you here – for that would take years! The theology of the Church is exceptionally complex, first because its divine character is entirely embodied in a human society, second because one cannot understand the Church without understanding how it developed historically. One is constantly running into problems at the institutional level, concerned with the Church's rights and prerogatives. To understand what we can, therefore, is all the more important, since today more than ever before we need that rock on which our faith is built.

Jesus made it very clear that his Church would be subject to temptation. It would have to endure hard and frequent shocks. We must not be alarmed when these occur; we do all we can to deepen and strengthen our faith in the Church. I should like to be able to help you to do this. As religious, you are founded in the Church. Your consecration, above all your perpetual profession, is an act by the Church. You are at the Church's service, for no one can be at Christ's service without being at the Church's service too.

The question therefore arises: How in practical terms are you to reconcile your faith in the Church with the difficulties, objections and painful choices with which you are familiar, especially those arising from political decisions to be made? The Church is complex by virtue of being a completely human, sociological, historical and political entity, in the general sense that it cannot help being this. History is there to prove it. On the one hand, you have the scandal of social injustice. On the other, you have the law of humility and the way of revealed truth: and this has to be extended and deepened, even though entrusted to the feeble resources of the people trying to preserve it in its purity. A bond, you might say a mysterious union, exists between the Church as the organised community of the faithful, and the Kingdom of God, hidden in the present world already, yet the coming of which we still await. Once again, I have to use the word mysterious, since it is the only one suitable for designating an invisible reality largely defying human understanding and hence impossible to express in any depth.

Christ always spoke of his Church in this dual perspective: as the site of the Kingdom of God already present among his followers. In the parables there are constant allusions to this awaited reality, to which Christ directed the faith of the first Christian community, as also towards the second coming of Christ and the complete realisation of the Kingdom. So we must not lose sight from now on of the fact that the Church is more than the sum of its earthly organisation and that it constantly transcends whatever it can accomplish here-below.

At a time when a more generalised, more violent and more pernicious attack is being mounted against the Church than ever before, one of the most important acts of the Second Vatican Council has been to offer an updated and very comprehensive definition of what the Church is and ought to be. We should, in my view, be failing in our duty as sons of the Church, were we not to ponder over these Conciliar documents: for these should be thoroughly absorbed by the faithful both to renew their outlook and clarify their concept of the Church, both to strengthen each member's own Christian faith and to induce new patterns of behaviour in the Church's members and clergy as a whole.

As far as we are concerned, there is one point in particular which I should like to stress: that we should have a complete vision of the mystery of the Church as regulator of our faith. The Church authenticates our religious life, receives our consecration, mediates our obedience to Christ,[32] makes obedience possible and gives it practical content, without which it would be no more than a general attitude of mind with no concrete effect in our lives. Claiming to obey Christ by doing in fact what we have made up our own minds to do would be a cut-rate, delusive sort of obedience. No, an attitude presupposing the presence of Christ in the Church cannot be divested of all mystery. But this does not prevent obedience from being translated into concrete and often difficult relationships over practical matters between individual fraternities and the local Church as represented by its pastor. At this level, above all, we must stay in communion with the Church.

How deserving of criticism the Church often seems to be! What weaknesses, what limitations! And hence, what strictures levelled against it from top to bottom! Yes, this is how the mystery presents itself to us, putting our faith and reason to a severer test than any other Christian mystery does. What indeed, to the eye of reason, is the Church? What is it to unbelievers? What is the Church to a marxist analysing history? How does the Church appear to a historian, if not as a human society with its own personnel and fairly complicated organisation, often affecting somewhat anachronistic forms, and the dignitaries of which in comparatively recent times used to make their public appearances dressed in lace, observing the fashion of some two centuries earlier? In it, the historian would also detect a mentality formed in a virtually closed environment, the ecclesiastical environment. Like all environments, this one uses a more or less private language; it is characterised by political attitudes insufficiently abreast of the times.[33] But there is no point in elaborating on what everyone knows and keeps repeating, all too often without making qualifications and not without misrepresenting the facts. For the dignitaries of the Church are after all only men like ourselves, though they have heavy moral and spiritual responsibilities to bear. Religious, priests, and even certain bishops are not immune to ambition, jealousy, spiritual pride, opportunism, love of temporal power and social influence: these features are all found within the Church. In the course of history, there have been schisms, heresies, theological disputes evincing little respect either for truth or for people. Attitudes taken by the Church or by such and such an episcopate may now seem out of date and discredited in the light of new situations. The most impartial historian could not overlook the Holy See's abuse of its temporal power, nor the moral corruption ravaging the Papal Court at certain periods in the past. Glittering wealth, patronage and encouragement of the arts, immense building projects, all emphasised the temporal aspect of the Pope's political power. This is all true: no one is denying it, so we can leave it at that.

In our own day, a pitilessly critical gaze keeps the Church in turmoil from within. For the Church has come to question itself. On the one side, leftists and progressives, on the other, traditionalists and integrists, each claiming to be right and the other wrong. And when you read a theological treatise, you find the Church portrayed as Bride of Christ, the Heavenly Jerusalem, the City of God, holy without wrinkle or blemish . . . What are believers, the everyday faithful, to make of it all?

So a yearning rises in Christian hearts for a Church as it used to be in the days of Jesus, when poor Simon Peter fishing in his lake, and the other apostles, had neither power nor money. Yet how misleading, this unrealistic vision of the past! If you have been living in those days, what wouldn't you have found to criticise! Those uneducated people, ignorant of everything outside their narrow Galilean world, would certainly have struck you as politically backward. And yet they had the presumption to preach Christ to a cultured Greek society, with no other preparation than their personal attachment to Jesus. You would very likely have noted the somewhat unacceptable character of Peter with his limited outlook, and would have been disappointed by the arguments taking place between the apostles. They too had their limitations and weaknesses, and made mistakes. Bishops, not excluding the Pope, are all marked by a culture, a language, an accent. They, like other men, are subject to anxiety, discouragement, weariness, defects of age, whether old age or youth. So where is the Church in all this?

In the eyes of the unbeliever or historian, the Church is a very ancient institution with a history of ups and downs corresponding to the fluctuations of human civilisation. Seen like this, the Church may seem an admirable institution in more respects than one. It is the only institution, for instance, to have remained itself throughout the centuries and to have survived the crash of empires, changes in government, cultural crises. Some people will say that it is the last example of monarchical government and still retains a number of its trappings. It is not very long since the Sovereign Pontiff gave up wearing his tiara of three crowns: one of these symbolising supreme temporal power and the right to enthrone and depose emperors and kings.

Christians today react against this aspect of the Church and sometimes go so far as to arraign the very institution itself. They want a humble, poor, serving Church, without always being precisely aware how these requirements are to be met in a society as vast as modern Christendom. Yes, indeed, we can see the need for radical change in the myriad institutions through which the modern Papacy wields its power. A complicated centralised administration, a canon law in a state of flux and many articles of which are now considered out of date: all this, we foresee, will have to change. But then, where will the fixed point be? When and how will Peter's power be exercised? – charged as he is to strengthen his brothers' faith. The Church can only be reformed by light and force of faith; other means can only be destructive. The activities of St Catherine of Siena spring to mind. At a time when the Papacy was in a deplorable state, the successor of Peter having fled from Rome with his court, Catherine set off to find him, forcefully reproved him and bade him return to Rome. Yet she, the while, was motivated by deep respect for the man whom she called her '*sweet Christ on earth*'. What a force for truth and freedom faith unleashed in this young woman, who was prepared to confront the mystery of her Church and not to be scandalised by what was routinely human in it – by what could not but be human in it – while she never ceased to contemplate the divine reality hidden at the core of that more or less frivolous and political court of the Avignonese pontiffs! Could Christ have constituted his Church in any other way, without confounding the effects of the Incarnation? Is Christ still present in the Church of today, impugned as it is by so many? Is the Holy Spirit still at work in the Church?

Our period is, after all, only one stage among many others

ın the Church's lengthy history, nor will it be the last. Contemplating the Church in its representatives, in its *personnel* as Jacques Maritain called them, we find that the Church is no worse and no better than it was in the past or is likely to be in the future: for men will always be men, subject to sin, prone to error and narrowmindedness, limited by partial but invincible ignorance.

So I wonder whether we don't risk shaking our faith, when we uncritically add our own voices to the chorus of the Church's critics. And heaven knows, we do not always hold back! And so it comes about that many of the faithful lose their faith in the Church. They lose confidence in it. What the Church teaches, what the Church says, no longer commands the hearing and understanding which it should. The silence which has fallen since the Council – a silence itself criticised by many people – betrays the Church's own awareness that its teachings can no longer be imposed by an act of authority. Its teachings can only be received by the humble, faithful heart; in other respects, the Word of God can no longer make itself heard in the voice of the Church.

In the present state of human thought and theological research, it is no use denying the difficulties which exist in determining when the Church is making a demand on our faith. Where and how does what is called the *magisterium* of the Church express itself? When Paul VI says a word or two to an audience of pilgrims, he does not always speak in his capacity of guardian of the faith. One may well feel in disagreement with what he says; or realise that he is not properly informed. The Pope cannot always be delivering himself as Supreme Pastor of the Church; this above all, when the subject in question pertains to mixed topics, to politics for instance, in which religion is only indirectly concerned. On these occasions, it is not always easy to reconcile the respect due to his person and the humble and attentive faith in which his teachings and directives ought to be accepted, with the individual Christian's lawful right to use his own judgment and act according to his conscience in all matters except those within the doctrinal domain.

We must have the simplicity, good sense and faith to accept the deeper meaning of the mystery of the Incarnation. And this is not such an easy thing to do! We are often tempted into a kind of supernaturalism, into demanding irrefutable Gospel signs that God is with us; or indeed, if we do not find these, to hesitate and argue, and then we get bogged down in the merely human aspect of things. And what are we left with, then?

When the Word became flesh and Jesus appeared in history, he founded a mission universal in time and space. The mission is an eschatological one, in the sense that it is never finished, ever marching towards a future dictating the line of advance but forever eluding us. Jesus effected this mission by first inaugurating the coming of the Kingdom of God and then by founding the Church. And the mission, being by nature universal, had to be capable of indefinite prolongation throughout history. Now, Jesus only spent thirty-two years on earth; his preaching was limited to the confines of Galilee and Judaea and in fact was only accepted by a small number of people, even in those fleeting hours when the crowds, excited by his miracles, flocked round him wanting to proclaim him as Messianic King. Their enthusiasm was soon cut short, when Jesus refused the temporal mission offered him and when the promises about the Kingdom, interpreted in terms of immediate fulfilment, did not come true. When he was condemned by the national authorities and put to death on the cross, the crowds had almost completely lost interest in him. Even the apostles evinced the same loss of faith. '*Our own hope had been that he would be the one to set Israel free. And this is not all: two whole days have gone by since it all happened.*'[34] The disciples' disappointment was complete. Their hopes had been dashed to pieces.

If the Word truly did become flesh, this event must necessarily affect all ages. And how was it to be effective for all time? We have to grasp what God's plan was about. What the Incarnate Word proclaimed, what he revealed about the Name of God, what he achieved by his death and ressurrection: how was all this to be presented to all men for all ages to come? How did Christ propose to continue his mission? How was Christ to reach the hearts of men as yet unborn? How was his Eucharist – that final gift bestowed in a few words on his apostles before he died – to be handed down and perpetuated to the end of time? How was he to go on uttering those words

of forgiveness and compassion which turned human lives upside down and rekindled hope? How was he to answer men's
questionings about the meaning of their lives and their eternal
destiny? How was the Kingdom of God to advance in men's
souls and remain uncontaminated amid the flood of temptation and error? In the world which Christ had overcome, how
was the community of his followers to survive and faithfully
preserve what he had entrusted to them? You have only to
consider the transitory nature of human communities and
associations to see how hard it is for them to keep a common
ideal intact. So what do you give for the chances of faithfully
preserving a message as fragile, as deep, as mysterious as that
distilling from the words of Jesus? And especially now that
Jesus is not here anymore – I mean, in the sense that he no
longer intervenes through those modes of communication and
action which are normal to human societies.

The Church is a direct product of the Incarnation of the
Word, and by virtue of this is subject to the very law of the Incarnation. By the Incarnation, human nature became divine,
yet the Word, by becoming man did not change human
nature: he transfigured it. When I say that he did not change
it, I mean that the revelatory and active presence of God
permeated every aspect of human nature without the latter's
ceasing to be human or to exhibit any of the limitations
endemic to it. Jesus was man and was recognised as such by
his contemporaries. The union of the divine and human in
Christ was so intimate that his human nature both revealed
and veiled the transcendence of God. And insofar as it revealed it, this created an immense obstacle for the Jews. It is hard
for us to realise how difficult, how almost impossible, it was
for a Jew to recognise Christ as Son of the Most High. *Isn't he a
man? We know where he comes from. He comes from Nazareth. We
know his family.* His way of life and behaviour was so like
human behaviour! There was nothing startling about him, for
the transfiguration of the man in him was not to take place until after his resurrection. And then, by virtue of this, he would
no longer belong entirely to the world. The divine transfiguration of the man as Son was not of this world.

Thus, everything that God has to say to man here-below
passes through human nature and cannot come by other than
human means of communication. Otherwise there would have

to be a total reappraisal of the Incarnation, looking on this as
involving some kind of marvellous and visible transformation
of man; which in turn would involve a sort of contradiction
between the design of God the Creator and that of God the Incarnate. As though God, having made a number of mistakes
when originally creating man, had felt obliged to correct and
readjust his work by the Incarnation. For setting man free
from sin is something quite different. This does not involve
altering the nature of man, with all his natural limitations,
freedom, frailties on the one hand, and his accountability on
the other. Man is inescapably liable to make mistakes. The
consistency of God's plan is manifest in the fact that Christ's
appearance on earth has made no discernable alteration in the
over-all history of human behaviour.

So what could Jesus do after leaving this world: he who was
able to witness to the entire truth about his Father; he whom
no-one – to use his own words – could *'convict of sin'*,[35] who
could read the secrets of the human heart; who knew the roots
of sin in human nature and could consequently express God's
compassion for and confident understanding of his creatures,
born of him in his loving design? Yes, what could Jesus do to
make sure that his work would go on? Jesus could only live
one human life-span; such was the law of the Incarnation.
And yet the Paschal Mystery of death and life had already inducted mankind into a non-earthly world. The Risen Christ
could not continue acting as he had on earth; hence, on earth,
his message and mission were entrusted to the responsibility
of human beings. Jesus living in his Church is subject to those
means of communication normally obtaining in human
relationships.

I am sure we should have preferred a more direct and startling manifestation of the Divine Presence. For the transmission
of these truths by human agency is certainly a very slow
process at the mercy of the vicissitudes of human history.
From Galilee, the Good News had to pass to the neighbouring
peoples and cultures; there had to be journeys; people had to
get to know each other; the messengers had to learn another
language than their native tongue. These were the sort of
difficulties attendant on the spreading of the Gospel, as also
attendant on the Church chosen by God by virtue of the Incarnation. Any other way would have been a contradiction of the

Incarnation. yes, we might well have preferred a direct and plain revelation of God to every individual. But that would involve our admitting that God was transcending or transforming the normal laws governing human nature as created by him in the first place. Faith would have been something plain and easy and there would have been no need for the Church. But it would have meant the abolition of human nature too. God could not act like this, even if we find this difficult to admit. We see things in a simplistic way and shall always have a leaning towards the miraculous, towards *supernaturalism*, even in times dominated by scientific rationalism. When we look at human nature as revealed by its history and by its morality, we cannot help but be appalled! Faced with God's design, the human heart seems torn by conflicting desires: on the one hand, determined to have complete independence, and on the other, anxious to be other than it is!

I am not of course denying that God does in one sense intervene in the individual heart and conscience, but he does this without ever infringing the individual's freedom of choice. When St Paul was thrown to the ground on the road to Damascus, Christ did not tell him what to do then and there, but bade him go and find the Church in the person of Ananias. It was the latter's duty to tell Paul what to do. And thus Paul was to receive his mission from the Church. When a man is converted, knocked flat and enlightened by the Holy Spirit, the Church is the one he has to approach to find out what he should believe. The Church is the one to reveal to him the name of the Inexpressible One by whom he has been conquered.

Christ, we thus see, could not do without a human organisation, since human knowledge, science and wisdom itself are all and always transmitted though a structured society. Man cannot come to full intellectual or spiritual development except within the framework of a society. The Church is subject to the same means of transmitting its message as any other society is. For the Church to be able to transmit its message completely and perfectly, the members of this particular society who would actually have to transmit the message, would have to be perfect, supremely intelligent, enlightened and exempt from all possibility of error. They would in a word have to be supermen or angels! Yet we see from the evidence that Jesus did not in any respect alter Peter's temperament or abolish his limitations; nor did he do so for John, or for Paul, or for any of the other apostles, despite the graces which he bestowed on all of them. Christ chose these men, but took them and kept them as they were. The progress they made, their increasing fidelity to their mission, was to remain within the limits of what human beings can manage. Son of God as he was, the Messiah Saviour did not essentially change the human condition of his apostles. No, man is not a being whose creation has gone wrong. Wounded as he is by sin and needing to be cured, he is not a spoilt creation.

For the Church to be that society transfigured by the Gospel, radiant with truth and love, to which many believers aspire and which some insist that it ought to be, the human nature of its pastors and priests would have had to be transfigured to the point of being preserved from all faults and from all possibility of error. And the same too would have to go for every Christian, by virtue of his baptism. How lovely a Church like that would be! Our problems would all be over! The Church would be the radiant symbol of a new mankind. But this was not the plan of the Incarnation. This would have required a new creation, not in terms of Redemption but of escape from the earthly human condition.

This was not how Jesus wanted to pursue his mission. He founded the Church as we see it in history: a completely human society, yet ever supported as it lives and grows by the Almighty Spirit of Jesus, who is God, Spirit of God, so that, human weakness or even the faults and mistakes of its pastors notwithstanding, this Church is still able to prolong and contain Christ's own activity. This is an infinitely more divine achievement, given the omnipotence which it presupposes, than what would have amounted to refashioning mankind to other specifications than those in which we issued from the hand of the Creator.

The result of all this is, as you can see, that Christ is invisibly, inaccessibly, mysteriously present in his Church. The Church is Christ's body. Within itself, it contains that immense company of saints, by virtue of whom the Church is already founded and flourishing in that other world, the world of the Glorified Christ: the earthly Church making its painful way here-below, being but the smaller part of it. Such is the People of God, through whom the Kingdom of God is present among men. Obviously, if we could see the Church as it really is, if we could see not the outward behaviour and human organisation but the invisible aspect of the totality of individuals baptised into the Church, united by the same profession of faith and obedient to the one same shepherd; if we could read the secrets of the heart: then the Kingdom of God would appear to us as Christ himself sees it. As Père Journet, an expert on the theology of the Church, very rightly says: the frontiers of the Church do not run between man and man, dividing people into two groups; they run through each individual heart, in such a way that part of each individual's heart belongs to the Church and the other part does not. The frontiers of Christ's Church do not always coincide with those of the Kingdom of God.

There, in that invisible dimension of the Church, the Kingdom of God in the human heart, is where the Church is without blemish. For we cannot say the same of the Church's personnel. All Christians without exception, even churchmen, even saints, have faults. And people will never be satisfied with the Church's personnel. Christians or not, they will always have good reasons for criticising the Church as being in one way or other full of shortcomings and infidelities to the message which, these notwithstanding, it still has to convey. It sometimes takes a great deal of humility and self-sacrifice to stand four-square with the Church. The greatest obstacles which we encounter to absolute adherence to the mystery of the Church are spiritual pride and the paramountcy of reason. It can even happen that this pride lies at the root of apparently unexceptionable criteria, i.e. that the only Church that we ought to consent to accept should be one which is totally poor, totally just, totally comprehensive as regards human problems. This ideal and imaginary Church is so different from the one within our reach that it becomes a very obstacle, preventing us from adhering to the Church as it actually is. Now, of course, the Church would not be faithful to its calling, did it not arouse a constant effort towards progress and conversion on the part of its members and leaders. But a continually carping attitude to the Church cannot but weaken the bonds linking Christians to one another and to their pastors.

And gradual alienation can be the effect on those who, by criticising the Church too ferociously, eventually become unable to love and respect it. This notwithstanding, we must work boldly and tirelessly to change outlooks, institutions and hearts for the better, ever retaining a completely clearheaded and infinitely respectful faith in Christ's Church and its pastors, since Christ's face is there, disfigured as when he was climbing to Calvary. Such should be the Christian's faith.[36]

I should also like to emphasise the importance of the Church in heaven, for this, being complete and perfect, helps us to understand more about the Pilgrim Church on earth. The Church of our living dead and of the angels is the earnest of the coming of the future Kingdom. Christ, identified with his Church, in her continues to live the various stages of his Incarnation, his earthly life, his death and finally his resurrection, with the glorious transfiguration of human life implicit in this. It is very difficult for us to understand this mysterious aspect of the Church, in which we ourselves are members of Christ. The Church is well named the Body of Christ. When Jesus revealed himself to Paul on the road to Damascus, he identified himself with the infant Church which Paul was persecuting. '*Saul, Saul, why are you persecuting me?*'[37]

The Church as Body of Christ cannot be perceived except by faith. We cannot form a picture of what it really is. That is why there is such a very strong yet mysterious link between the Eucharist and the Church. In concrete terms and to outward appearances, the Eucharist, like the Church, is something very ordinary and wretched, all the more so since people are often at pains to make it more wretched still, whether by surrounding it with out of date and often tasteless ornaments, or by treating it with indifference and lack of respect. Yet, as a sign, the Eucharist summons us at the level of our behaviour as men. As does the Church. The Eucharist cannot exist without the Church and the Church cannot exist without the Eucharist. The Eucharist is the sign of Christ's presence in the Church. And we, as members of one another in a society subject to the laws of human solidarity, by means of the Eucharist are members of Christ. This hidden aspect of communion with the Church in heaven is something perhaps only perceived in the hearts of God's saints, in the Gospel meaning of the term: and by contemplation. When this living faith ceases to illuminate and govern our attitude towards the Church, we become to greater or lesser degree harmful to the unity of the Church of which we are members.

Although I cannot cover every aspect of the Church, I think it is important to say a little about the Church's faith. Nowadays, more than ever, we need to strengthen our faith, to become firmly convinced of it, so that it can illuminate our lives and allow us to give them unreservedly to the Church, by enabling us to attain the aims to which we are consecrated and for which we must be ready, if necessary, to lay down our lives in witness. If our faith is not secure, if it is only a feeling without real positive content, if it is disputed by our reason, then we are not ready to pledge our entire lives on it. No one hands his life over to a theory, no one gives his life for something in doubt. And if we do not give our lives, it is a waste of time to talk about consecration, for this is what consecration is all about. How are we to acquire a faith firm and assured enough as to become the goal and supreme rule of our lives? A faith made strong in the steadfastness of God can only be the very faith of the Church.

So, what is the Church's faith? When Jesus taught on earth – I mean not only what he actually said but what flowed from the manifestation of God in his person – he knew that all this would be the subject of reflection, of intense study, of discussion, leading to the elaboration of theological syntheses and ultimately to a coherent doctrine. It could not have been otherwise – or the disciples would not have been seriousminded people. It would be impossible for anyone to become intellectually aware of a truth as profoundly fundamental as the revelation of the Father in the Incarnation of the Son, without his having been impelled to make an effort to accept, understand and reflect on the verity thus revealed. For without such an effort, he would not have sufficient light by which to adapt his life to what had been revealed to him about his own mysterious destiny. Jesus was well aware of this. When he said one day that the Kingdom of God is like a mustard seed which is, when sown, 'the smallest of all the seeds on earth',[38] he was surely pointing out the disparity between the smallness of something as yet having no specific form, and the complexity of the living thing which would later emerge from it. If you were given a seed – a tiny little round thing – and asked to describe what it would germinate into, you would be quite unable to do so if you have never seen the plant in question, regardless of whatever scientific analyses of the seed you might choose to conduct. Now, the Kingdom was a unique seed, unknown to human experience. God alone could know what was to come out of it by continual, vigorous development: which development was in part entrusted to man's initiative, since man can produce conditions favourable to its germination and growth, can cut out the dead wood, can by pruning help it to develop and be fruitful. Man's collaboration is real, indeed essential, for the seed can die or the plant dry out for lack of care. But it is not within man's power to change the nature of the tree. At times, he may be able to stunt its growth, he may prune it clumsily or cut out the growing-tip, but he cannot actually prevent it from growing or alter the essential nature of the trees or of the fruit it has to bear. This is a good illustration of the way the Church is supposed to develop.

It is easily and often said that the Church should go back to what it was in the time of Christ. But this is to forget the fact that the Church of those days was no more than a seed entrusted to the apostles, and cannot be compared with what it has since developed into. In the time of Christ, the Church had not spread throughout the nations, had not encountered any of the problems presented by the human mind or by the various successive cultures to which the Church would have to adapt itself. The Church's faith would also have to meet the situation of the moment, and be able to guide the individual in his moral conduct. Thus, the Church took its form as it developed, just as the tree assumes unforeseen form as it rises from the seed. This is why a knowledge of history is so important if you want to understand the mystery of the Church. To redefine today's Church in terms of what that earliest of Christian communities conceived itself to be cannot be done. This would be like taking a seed, analysing it and claiming to describe what will grow out of it, when that seed is unique. We cannot forecast the design of the Church's architect. We are spectators as the work of the Holy Spirit progresses; and we have to let the Spirit instruct us, if we are to see the true face of the Church at each successive stage. Christ told Simon that he would be the rock on which the Christian Church was to be built. And there is nothing anarchic about the way the Church has developed, it is not disjointed, it is a living process, since it is as a living entity that the Church develops and expands on earth. The Church is alive with the life of the Body of Christ. Yet everything that is yet to come, including Christ's final coming in glory and the consequent fulfilment of the Kingdom, was initially contained in that seed entrusted to the apostles by Christ. Tresmontant it was, I think, who wrote that the Church when founded contained a genetic code. This is a new kind of Gospel parable, using the scientific terms of modern biology. We cannot alter the genetic code created by Christ, but we can collaborate constantly in fostering it.

No Christian can do without the Church, for to understand the full mystery of Christ we have to resort to the Church's memory, recording and preserving everything that its members, the saints, have experienced and been able to express of the insights conferred by the Holy Spirit, ranging from mystical contemplation to theological research, deepening our knowledge of the truth contained in the revealed Word of God. All this is the Church's faith. This is what is universal. This is what, we find, has been gradually assimilated, not by virtue of temporarily valid systems appropriate to this period or that, still less by what distinguishes or divides the various schools of theology, but by virtue of what particles of truth all these contain: and these particles of truth recognised as such by the Church are assimilated into the lively and growing structure of its faith and progressively enrich its treasury. Who instructs me in wisdom and experience of God, who guides me in these matters, is not this or that Biblical critic or such and such a theologian, but the Church.

But, you will say, who is to guarantee that the Church's faith is correct? How am I to recognise it amid the competing and often very disparate doctrines of today, and how am I to distinguish between a theological hypothesis advanced by some scholar or other and what actually constitutes the faith of the Church? This does indeed present one of the gravest problems of contemporary Christianity. There was a time when the teaching Church was sharply distinguished from the taught. The teaching Church was represented, as far as the faithful at large were concerned, by the priests speaking authoritatively from the pulpit and, more rarely, by a letter or directive from the diocesan bishop. Now, if the priests were the normally accredited mouthpieces of the Church, they nonetheless did not constitute the so-called Teaching Church. The latter consisted of the Sovereign Pontiff, bishops and, of course, General Councils. Everbody else, including theologians, were the taught. The faithful were only expected to listen and humbly accept the teaching given, the essential elements of which were summed up in the catechism. They did not question what the Church's faith actually was, even though they might have personal difficulties and doubts. Theological investigation was a matter for specialists, and the faithful at large were not kept informed about the problems which were being discussed. Doctrinal disputes, with the ensuing condemnations by Councils and the entering of books on the Index, took place at a level never affecting the general public. The orthodox faith was safeguarded from the influence of too adventurous speculation, imperilling the faith of the simple, of the poor, of people in no position to evaluate the import of such discussions, of people with no adequate means of countering the unsettling effects of such and such a famous Biblical scholar's opinions – today broadcast to all. Yes, today things are different. The wildest theological discussions and opinions, on occasion striking at the very fundamentals of the faith, are presented on television without any allusion whatever to what the orthodox teaching of the Church on the topic in question may be. Orthodoxy is virtually a forbidden word: people do not even dare to use it. So the question of what the Church actually does teach is a very material one indeed.

Looking at the Church of today, I feel at a loss unless I know something of its history. The Councils of time past, the doctrinal truths formulated long ago, no longer command interest. People do not know about them, or do not know properly about them, and in either case are convinced that they are now being questioned because they are no longer relevant to modern times. Free discussion, the so-called scientific investigations of Biblical scholars, new interpretations of the faith, the need for a new vocabulary, the adaptation of the faith to modern systems of philosophic thought, all breed con-

fusion for the believer, leaving him without landmarks or firm
footing. Whether on his own or in a group, how is he to find
out what the faith of the Church really is?

There is no doubt at all that we are going through a difficult
period. When St Paul alludes to people who let themselves be
carried away by every wind of doctrine, we understand exactly
what he means. Now, more than ever, if we accept God's
revelation of himself in his Son Jesus as our point of departure,
we need the Church's memory. Memory is, as it were, the
Church's eternal dimension. We cannot progress without a
spiritual memory. The Church's memory is intended to
refresh our individual memory. One of the Fathers of the
Church – I forget which – said that the Church journeys
through history like someone with eyes in front and in the
back of her head. The Church has eyes behind, because she
has to keep looking back to Christ and the apostolic age to
reconsider what was originally entrusted to her. She has eyes
in front because she is journeying through history, marching
towards the complete fulfilment of the Kingdom of God. The
Church's memory situates her outside time and gives her an
eternal dimension, in that she preserves the memory of
Christ's words which proclaim his second coming: in which
she believes and which she proclaims, and to the realisation of
which she is totally committed. Any attempt to deepen our individual faith must ultimately consist in our acquiring as
much of the content of the Church's memory as our own
memory can absorb.

Memory plays an essential part in our lives. It lifts us out of
the immediacy of the present to give our lives, even now, an
eternal dimension in terms of hope and expectation. By
memory, we overcome time. Memory makes our own past present to us, it allows us actually to hear Christ preaching to his
apostles. Thanks to memory, we can really enter the thoughts
of the apostles, the evangelists, the Fathers of the Church, of
St Irenaeus, St John Chrysostom, St John of the Cross. By
faith in the promises of Christ, we are kept mindful of Judgment Day, of our own deaths and of the coming of Christ. By
memory, we overcome time: it is a distinguishing attribute of
man. Man's eternal destiny is revealed to him by memory. St
John of the Cross writes of purifying the memory. I used to
wonder what he meant by this and found the idea difficult to

grasp: it was this – those who wish to journey towards God must purify what they remember of the things of God, must purge their memory of what is untrue, must purge it of unhealthy and depressing thoughts about past faults, of all worldly memories uselessly encumbering it and so preventing it from being available for God to use.

By memory, the Church identifies herself with the unfolding of the mystery of Christ in all its fulness; whatever she has to tell us comes out of her memory. This, you will tell me, is all very true and convincing, given a contemplative view of the Church; but in practice, as far as I am concerned, what am I to do to discover and tap the Church's memory? How, how is the Church's faith and authentic memory going to be expressed? To discover this, we should have to find a way of memorising what exactly was believed by the saints from the apostolic age, through the Fathers of the Church, right up to modern times. Vast libraries could hardly contain all that! And only a few privileged people have access to these. What are the people to do – the vast majority of the People of God – who have neither the means nor the time for such research? The answer most commonly given now is that they have the Gospel and that this is the essential thing and sufficient, with the aid of the Holy Spirit. Now we know perfectly well that this is not sufficient! And this is why we are obliged to admit that the faith of the People of God depends on the Church's organs of transmission. The proper transmission of the faith of the Church is the job and responsibility of her evangelists.

Hence Christ instituted the Church as a hierarchical body, each member having his own place and different function in it.[39] You yourselves have not been called to conduct theological research, you have not been called to set off down unknown paths with only yourselves to consider. You have been sent to the poor, to those humbly thirsting to receive unadulterated what Jesus came to teach them. This mission demands that your faith be complete, genuine, sure, and that you have made the effort to assimilate the Church's message, the Church's apostolic faith, in your memory as in your life. This requires preparation, this requires discipline, discipline imposed on our curiosity and our taste for novelty; this requires time devoted to study, and genuine intellectual humility. But this is another matter, what I shall not be dealing with here. Let us go back to the question of how the Church expresses her faith.

First of all, obviously, there is the Apostles' Creed, an abridgment of Christian doctrine, expressing the faith of the Church and People of God for the past twenty centuries. The Church needs to express or, more accurately, to bear witness to, her faith. A common outward profession of one faith is what unites the Church. As she journeys through the history of human thought, the Church has been constantly faced with the need to make new assessments. Yet, owing to the pressure of events, periods occur in the Church's life when she has not had time to form her assessments, the Church even in this task being subject to ordinary human limitations. The faster the changes occur, the greater the risk for the Church that her assessments will lag behind. Our own century is characterised by the unprecedented speed with which successive systems, doctrines and scientific findings have been produced, and this makes it particularly difficult for the Church to keep abreast of her task of assessing new situations, as also of her task of assessing what degree of truth resides in the welter of contemporary theology. Hence, the faithful are indeed at present at the mercy of every doctrinal breeze, influenced by the personality of the last preacher, priest or theologian to utter, or by the latest book to appear on the bookstalls.

I often think of what Christ said when standing with all the little children round him. '*Anyone causing the fall of one of these little ones who have faith, would be better thrown into the sea with a great mill-stone round his neck*'.[40] What terrible words! Be careful what you say. Think before you speak, especially before criticising what the Church stands for. Do not let yourselves veer with every wind of doctrine, reading whatever is in fashion, giving equal weight to every latest theory; for the risk of shaking our faith, of tarnishing it, of disfiguring it, is there for all of us. Systematic criticism of the Church cannot but undermine the integrity of the faith. Yes, Christ's warning should be taken very seriously. Since we have to bear witness to the faith, we have a heavy responsibility to bear as regards the People of God and particularly as regards the lowliest, those preferred by Jesus, the poor. They have the right to hope, by virtue of absolute faith in Christ; and hence they have the right to believe in the Church and to trust in her. Without her, their faith would soon be shaken and wounded unto death.

Are we likely to emerge unscathed from these sterilising arguments about the faith? Isn't it better to risk – you always risk something, whatever you do – having people tax you with being traditionalists, rather than to expose yourselves to the risk of undermining one or other aspect of other people's faith in the Church? There is another danger too: that of not helping the personnel of the Church to transcend themselves and to give a more evangelical quality to the way they serve the People of God. I don't think we can ever be perfect in this respect. When I give retreats for the laity, some people tell me that I am a *progressive*. Others, however, think that I am an *intergrist*. To them I say that I am neither one nor the other, that I never think of things in those terms, that I try to be a son of the Church and that I believe that there is one truth, to which we ought to be faithful; furthermore, that I find a grain of truth now with one party, now with the other. My judgment is certainly fallible, I may well make mistakes, but I try to be loyal to the Church.

Then people ask: But how and when is the Church infallible in matters of faith; when does she proclaim those Gospel truths of which she is the guardian? To which I reply that, for our own times, we have the teachings of the recent Ecumenical Council. People seem to forget this. In a difficult period like ours, an Ecumenical Council is a supreme manifestation of the Church's teaching function. I refer you to the pronouncements of the Second Vatican Council. Where better would you find the truths of God and Jesus Christ? Where could you be better instructed in matters usually inaccessible to the enquiring mind? Since the Council, the Church's voice has grown more discreet, people say. Perhaps too rigid a statement of the Church's teachings might make the Church's teaching mission more difficult to carry out? Maybe. But there are other reasons, you may be sure. The acceleration of theological studies is such that there is no time to assimilate and assess. And I am very aware of the responsibility the Fraternity has of assessing, for if we are to transmit the faith held by the Church to people thirsty for God, we must be competent to do this. This is our responsibility. How are we to discharge it faithfully?

I sincerely hope that you will take your theological studies very seriously indeed – not pursuing them to satisfy your intellectual curiosity about some given topic, but to help you perform your mission as you should. Given, however the present situation as regards theological research, you must realise that it will not be easy to find answers totally consistent with the Church's memory and at the same time totally appropriate to the problems of our own day. We have to grasp the fact that the choices we make in this matter are very serious ones. We must be humble and clear-headed enough to realise that we are not invulnerable at that level where intellect conditions faith, and to resist the tendency to believe that, in the ultimate analysis, it is up to the individual to decide on what is appropriate and what is not. Now, the gift of insight is not ours – outside or in opposition to the Church, that is. It is often all too easy to be of the same opinion as the last author one has read, particularly if he is an intelligent man, as usually is the case. It is easy to be convinced by some new, scientific approach to Biblical studies, for instance, or by some new and attractive interpretation of the Christian message, put forward in the light of history or modern philosophy. But you will easily lose your bearings in this, and your faith consequently will be the more confused and uncertain.

The question to be answered is this: whether, given respect for the personal responsibility of each Little Brother, the choice of studies and even of reading-matter should be left to the judgment and free choice of the individual? I think it should not. For this is a sphere in which both Church and Fraternity have a right to speak. Be the importance of theological research and renewal what it may, this must not only encourage our total adherence to the Church's faith but must also be consistent with our vocation. Our desire to study must be rooted in love, must spring from the need to know and make known more about the object of our love. Our mission is not to conduct theological investigations, nor to lose ourselves in studies likely to deprive our witness among the People of God of that simplicity and firmness which it ought to have.

We must not stop believing that the Church of today is the Church of forever, Christ's Church, and that even now the Church is the firm rock of our loyalty to God. It is the duty of the Prior and other responsible persons to decide what theological studies should be pursued, for these studies have a serious bearing on the whole concept of religious life, the purpose of contemplative prayer and our mission as evangelists. In this matter, what we need in the Fraternity is to develop a common awareness and sense of real co-responsibility about keeping faithful to our vocation. Faithfulness to the faith of the Church is hard to maintain at the intellectual level, and obedience is all too easily evaded. For when human reason clings to what it believes to be the truth, no authority, not even the highest, can do anything about it. There is only one form of obedience applicable to the intellect and this is what is very properly called obedience of faith. Whatever our personal opinions may be, our human intellect must bow before all truths that we conceive to be of divine origin. The act of believing involves the abandoning of our intellect to Christ. Now, it happens that we cannot abandon it to Christ except through the Church. Otherwise, who would attest the divine origin of what is offered to our faith? Once again, I know I am touching on a difficult question which cannot be treated in isolation. Theologians may dispute over it. But the mass of the faithful, the workers and the poor, cannot do more than put their trust in 'those who know and bear witness'.

So your studies and reading programmes must not be anarchic. The disorders in some religious communities, leading in some cases to their ruin, are sometimes due to a too absolute faith having been put in such and such a theologian, who teaches a doctrine unduly slanted by his personal researches and insufficiently co-ordinated to the faith of the Church. This is what we mean by saying that research can be anarchic. And research is all the more complex, now that the notion of theology has swollen to the point of laying claim to embrace every department and activity of human life, including most particularly politics and political activities.

So we in the Fraternity must be prepared to bear a joint responsibility for everything that concerns the understanding of the faith in the present world and particularly in the environment of the poor. And this is a very grave responsibility, as you must be aware. We cannot solve this problem simply by leaving every brother free to read and study whatever he pleases, and consequently to make his personal choices in matters philosophical and ideological. This would merely be deceiving ourselves about human mentality and human weakness. We turn into what we read; in the long run we are influenced by a human environment, if we accept it hook, line and sinker. This is an inevitable law. So, you will tell me, we are to be brainwashed? Yes, we are going to be brainwashed, there is nothing else for it! If the marxist has the right to brainwash himself by studying marxism-leninism and by immersing himself completely in a given ideological environment, having chosen to be loyal to orthodox marxism-leninism, we too, as Christians, have the same right to condition ourselves to be loyal to the orthodox presentation of our faith. For there is an orthodoxy, say what you may, since there is a way of reaching the Truth. A marxist, believing himself to be right – I take marxism as an example but I might equally well take any other ideology instead – considers it right and normal that he should have the right to impose his way of seeing and doing things on others. By the same token, we believe that Jesus Christ has borne witness to certain truths about God, human destiny and the Church, so why should we too not do all we can to make sure we do not lose this faith, most particularly since we know that it is frail, frail because it is not reinforced and confirmed by an immediate ability to produce tangible results?

In conclusion, I should like to say a word about the reign of the Holy Spirit. It is a fact that our own times are characterised by particular manifestations of the Spirit and by a proliferation of gifts attributed to him. Perhaps we ought to see these facts as a compensation, as a comfort, for Christians in the complex and difficult times for the Church which we have been describing. The opposition encountered by the Church is not only directed against her temporal organisation or against the institutions of the Vatican – for these are structures which, being relative, can always be overhauled – but more radically against her very teaching and against the traditional expression of the faith. We live in times when the need for the Holy Spirit's gift of discernment has never been more acute.

What then is this discernment conferred by the Holy Spirit? When Jesus sent the breathing of the Spirit on his apostles at

Pentecost, he founded the Church. The reign of the Spirit therefore cannot be regarded as something dissociated from the Church or from the teachings of Jesus Christ. The Holy Spirit cannot be genuinely manifested outside or in competition with Christ living in his Church, or even in competition with the hierarchy of that Church, that is to say, with those members of the People of God who have been invested by this same Spirit, their personal shortcomings notwithstanding, with the responsibility of governing Christ's disciples and of strengthening their loyalty to the faith. It is the same Spirit acting in all: quite contrary to the current tendency to dissociate the reign of the Spirit from the activities of the Church as now established, as though, the latter having become unable to perform her mission, the Spirit had to supply the deficiency by bringing a new, parallel Church into existence, a living, more evangelical, more spiritual community and, above all, one without organisational structures! Admittedly, in small-scale, spontaneous communities, the Holy Spirit can re-vitalise prayer, evangelical energy, brotherly love and a sense of faith. But if a community of this sort does not share the faith of the Church, or if it refuses to acknowledge the authority of the Church's pastors, you can be sure that the Holy Spirit is not at the soul of such a movement. The Spirit of Jesus cannot work against himself. The Spirit of Discord often takes the form of an angel of light; Jesus foresaw that the spirit of discord and *'the Gates of Hell'*[41] would try to shake the foundations of his Church. It is taking rather too simple a view of things to attribute everything that happens now, when Christians meet to pray or to share the Word of God, to the action of the Holy Spirit. The religiosity inherent in attributing judgments, plans and decisions to the intervention of the Holy Spirit, when in fact they are the results of our own initiative and taken on our own responsibility, runs counter to the present secularising trend, which rightly emphasises the freedom of the human will within its own domain. We must not forget, even so, that the Holy Spirit is always at work among the People of God. Since the creation of mankind, the Spirit of God has been at work in men's hearts, in each individual heart. Since Jesus spoke and the Word of God was revealed to the world, we need the Spirit of the Lord, for us to understand that Word, and we need to be strengthened by that Spirit, so as to have the courage to be faithful to that Word. The reign of the Spirit of God did not begin today. In the past, people talked of the gifts of the Holy Spirit; now, they talk of the reign of the Spirit: but they are still talking about the same thing.

The confusion afflicting many people in their search for a higher way of life encourages them to seek light and strength in supernatural manifestations. By the same token, there is a tendency for us not to make a clear enough distinction between what lies within the province of our more or less conscious decisions, and what is truly an inspiration from the Holy Spirit. Do not be too easily led into believing that your path will be strewn with inspirations from the Holy Spirit! For that would end in a kind of self-abdication. God has made us free and intelligent, so that we can use our intelligence and freedom: not but what this will require painful effort and even involve the risk of making misjudgments. Only deep down within this search, within this effort, at the heart of your freedom, is the Spirit at work, helping you and enlightening you in so far as you are disposed to receive the Spirit's promptings in humility, and to adhere to the Church. It is not enough to have heartily invoked the Holy Spirit for your conduct to be inspired by him. Everything will depend on your inner dispositions before God. Even under the influence of his Spirit, we do not stop being responsible for ourselves. Mary was free to consent or not consent to the most exceptional work of the Spirit of God. If we are faithful, if we humbly try to put the Gospel into practice, to obey the Church, to adhere to the faith of the Church and to spread the Word, we shall be ceaselessly accompanied by the action of the Holy Spirit and shall remain under his influence.

However, when people talk about what are now called charisms, they usually have particular manifestations of the Spirit in mind. In the Church, there have been and there are unexpected, unpredictable, transitory manifestations of the Holy Spirit, which are different from the invisible and more usual help which he confers. These charisms are bestowed to serve the community and they are always outward signs, even when they involve deep inward changes in those who receive or witness them. What the Apostle Paul said of the charisms of the churches of his day seems to be happening again in our own. On the right way to receive them and integrate them into the life of a Christian community, I cannot but refer you to the words of the Apostle himself.[42] We must not seek or desire these charisms for themselves, and when they do occur, they can have no other ultimate purpose than the building up of charity and unity. They should lead us back to the Church and make us into more active, more lively, more enlightened members of it, and not promoters of vain discussion and division. If anyone fleetingly receives such a gift, let him not pride himself on it. We must not forget that the Church as a whole can be regarded as an institutional charism – although this may seem a contradiction in terms. The charism of enlightenment, of fidelity, resides in the totality of the Church and particularly in the Sovereign Pontiff when he speaks as universal pastor, as also in the college of bishops. Continual help has been promised them by Christ,[43] so that they can guide the flock without leading it astray, even despite occasional deviation, miscalculation and inadvertant clumsiness.

Religious life, at its well-springs, is charismatic too. When God raises a man or a woman to inaugurate a new current of Christian life and spirituality, he acts in such a way that, through providential situations, by radiance of holiness and by the obvious originality of a new type of Christian life, the exemplar will give birth to a congregation of religious who will copy him and take him for their guide. The sum of this action and the individual calls associated with it constitutes a charismatic manifestation. The fact that a saint gives birth to a spiritual posterity renewing itself from one generation to the next always implies a free and unpredictable intervention by the Holy Spirit. Without that intervention and the permanent force for renewal which it contains, religious life would be irremediably subject to the gradual degeneration which time infallibly imposes on human institutions.

I hope that in very humble loyalty to the Spirit dwelling in your hearts, dear sons of God and brothers of Christ, you will take pains to foster within yourselves a love as great for the Church as that evinced by St Catherine of Siena: a lucid and yet infinitely respectful love, a love which builds and does not destroy; a love which tends to unite and not divide; a love which generates progress and renewal in the personnel of the Church and her institutions, yet refuses to scandalise the lowly and poor. This attitude of mind and will is hard to maintain, for very often and sometimes unwittingly we shall be tempted, out of human respect, to echo others' facile criticisms. We may also feel obliged, as a matter of principle, to side with unbelievers or those inclined to criticise the Church on political or ideological grounds. Without always realising what we are doing, we may thus be contributing to depriving people of the only factor capable of maintaining the frail light of a faith which, though quite defenceless against the force of reason, is the only thing able to open hearts to the knowledge of Christ, of eternal life and of the Church – for without the Church, that light would fade and die.

VII

The Evangelistic Mission and its Political Implications

In this talk I shall be dealing with our mission as evangelists and with some specific situations in which this mission will have to be performed. By now I hope you are firmly convinced that, by agreeing to join the Fraternity of the Gospel, you have in fact consented to put yourselves entirely at the Lord's disposal, in the intention of carrying out a call from him which consecrates you to the evangelist's task. As the name of our Fraternity bears witness, you are Little Brothers of the Gospel or, to put it in another way, Little Brothers of the Good News.

For Jesus son of Mary, the accomplishing of this mission was the reason for his existence as Christ. As he himself said, just as he had himself been sent by the Father, so he was sending his disciples and the whole Church to continue that mission, so that the Good News would eventually permeate the hearts of all mankind and the Kingdom of God gradually take shape. Now, although the mission concerns the whole Church and each of her members, the Lord has chosen some individuals to be full-time, life-long evangelists. I say life-long advisedly, since the lives of these envoys of the Lord will be so affected by the task that they will only be able to discharge it at great cost to themselves by sacrificing their earthly lives to it – and even dying for it. For the evangelistic mission is such that even for Christians who have not been specially singled out for the task, in a sense it commits them for life. I do not mean a propagandist mission or even a straightforward teaching one, which definite, limited activities could discharge; I mean the witnessing by life and word to everything revealed and accomplished by the Word of God on earth. You know all this already and I need not go into it further, except to remind you of the significance of the state to which your profession of chastity, poverty and obedience now commits you, since that state of life is to be regarded as a real identification with Christ's state, and as emphasising the vital union existing between these three aspects of Christ's life, all three being interdependent.

Christ could not have not been chaste, poor and obedient, as he in fact was. The unifying factor of his whole life, the basic motivation of his awareness as man, was, as the evidence shows, the obedience of the Suffering Servant, the readiness of the envoy to do whatever He who sends him requires, the total abandonment of the Son to the Father begetting him and charging him with a mission on earth. The Son never stops looking at the Father and, in his own words, *he always does what pleases him.* Jesus goes even further and says that the Father is acting in him and that he *can do nothing by himself, but only what he sees the Father doing.*[44]   In performing that mission, Christ is as though totally absorbed by the demands of a twofold love: the love he has for his Father, and love for his fellow-men. For the mission can only be discharged in terms of this twofold love. The unity of his life resides in this. And so, to be totally obedient to his mission, he could not be other than chaste and poor. For him, celibacy and poverty were not the refusal or rejection of a positive good. To take the loving, unified personality of a poor, chaste Christ to pieces, to examine his chastity as a separate factor and acclaim it in the abstract as a virtue might not be wrong perhaps, but would surely prevent us from reaching any deeper understanding of Christ's state. We cannot separate this aspect of his personality from the rest of his behaviour or from the love animating his whole existence. Similarly, his poverty could not be – least of all – considered separately. For this is a way of looking at things, a supreme detachment, a way of being affecting his every relationship with the world of things. How can we reduce Christ's poverty to nothing more than an economic or even social aspect of his life? It would indeed be disfiguring Christ's poverty to regard it as mere privation of wealth, of comfort, of social success. For in fact it is the reflection, as regards the world and creatures, of the supreme reality of the Kingdom of God and the contemplation of things eternal, this being his ruling preoccupation. The universal spiritual fertility of his personality as Saviour expressed itself thus in the way he lived on earth, by chastity and poverty. I shall not go over this again, since we have already said enough about it. But

since I am dealing with the evangelist's mission, I had to remind you that joining in that mission involves the whole life of
anyone called to do so. And this is why there is such a very
close link between your mission and the way you live. Your
consecration is a total consecration both to that mission and of
yourselves to Jesus, to serve him with a love asking no return.

What Jesus proclaims and what the evangelist serving him
passes on is something quite new. The way the message is
passed on also raises a problem as to the personal salvation of
those who do not hear that Good News, for it is passed on very
slowly, with long delays and many imperfections, through the
channels of the Church, by human means of communication
which are the only ones the Church can use, such being her
Founder's intention.

What is proclaimed and passed on is Good News and it is
something new that people would not be able to find out for
themselves. Left to themselves, how could people discover that
the Word became flesh and that in him God opened the infinite fulness of his intimate life of light and love to mankind? –
yes, with the prospect of resurrection and new life! They could
not possibly do so; even if, feeling their way by the dim light
of their highest imaginable spiritual intuitions, some have
reached the point of desiring an eternal destiny of the sort.

I should like to digress for a moment. Since the question is
put, we must be clear in our minds just what we are talking
about – not so much the personal salvation of each and every
human being, but rather the fact of proclaiming Jesus Christ.
Let me make myself clear. Faced with the impenetrable
mystery of how the eternal salvation of the individual occurs,
we can only keep silent and trust to the compassion of the
Father, whose love for each one of his creatures knows no
bounds. The mystery of universal individual salvation is not
what primarily lies at the root of the evangelistic mission, but
the fact that Jesus wishes to be revealed to men and that the
Kingdom of God, founded by him, must go on growing and
developing until its eschatological fulfilment. Far from being
irrelevant to the salvation of the individual, the revealing of
Christ the Saviour and of Christ's Kingdom embodied in the
mystery of the Church is of supreme importance for
everybody, even for those people who will never hear about
Christ here-below.

We have a very limited view of things, which makes us raise questions which we are not in fact in a position to solve. yet we should like to know everything, we should like to foresee everything and to organise everything cleanly and efficiently. And so we feel a need to know how, in what circumstances and on what conditions, a man may hope to win what is called his eternal salvation. Theologians have raised these questions. They have even tried to determine the degree of knowledge about God needful for someone if he is to be saved in the after-life, given that through no fault of his own it has not been possible for him to know and encounter Christ here-below. How can we even ask such a question? We have only to meditate on the parable of the Prodigal Son or on the way Christ treated the woman taken in adultery, to see that between God and the individual exists a mystery of love and compassion beyond our power to plumb. But if indeed this is the case, doesn't this tend to diminish the importance of our mission as evangelists and make it seem almost unnecessary? What is the point of evangelising people? Wouldn't it be better after all to let people go their own way, in harmony with their environment, comforted by their ancestral beliefs – trusting to their good-faith and high-mindedness and above all to the mercy of their Heavenly Father and Creator?

Christ's view of the creation, however, is much more powerful and complete than ours. He forcefully expressed his wish to be revealed as Saviour, and it is not for us to understand the relationship existing between the mystery of Christ and the salvation of each and every man who does not know him explicitly. This relationship nonetheless exists, in the same way as it existed between the revelation of Christ as Saviour when he lived on earth and the generations who lived in the centuries long after his coming. Everything to do with human destiny is contained in the mystery of Christ, and this mystery has to be spread throughout mankind; it has to progress towards accomplishment and grow towards a more and more complete submission of all creatures to the Universal Kingdom of Jesus.

The Kingdom of God was embodied in a people: Israel, during the period of gestation; and the Church, after the revelation of Christ. But the Kingdom of God exists for the salvation of each member of this people, while at the same time it consists of the whole body of the People of God at its most universal. Hand yourself over to Christ, understand that he is asking you to work for the extension of his revelation, and that this work is so important that you will have to give up your whole being and existence to it, for you to accomplish it by love, in faith, without distinction of persons and never denying it as against the world, even when the work sometimes seems utterly alien to the preoccupations of your contemporaries Because your Lord has called you, the evangelistic mission should be the ruling, nay, the unique concern of your life, and the constant preoccupation underlying your every decision and action; it should dominate everything and be the unique inspiration of what you think, what you wish and what you choose. For so it was for Jesus while he lived.

What demands then does this mission make and what forms does it take? By nature, the evangelist's mission is all-embracing, in the sense that it concerns the whole man in his present life and in his future one. It is all-embracing in its demands on the person who consents to discharge it, since it consists of a message which has to be lived by the person who hands it on. The message being a living message, you cannot proclaim it if you do not live it; and this is why we have said that it cannot be reduced to propaganda or even to something taught. It is possible to give lectures in theology without moulding one's life to Christ's message. It is possible for someone to proclaim Christ and not live by his message, but the possibility is a contradiction in terms, since the very content of that message is a call to change one's life. And this indeed is one of the factors on which the credibility of the messenger depends. How can you ask other people to pray if you do not pray yourself? How can you ask people to love one another, to be reconciled in love, if you do not yourself do everything you can to do the same, and if you do not feel humbled at the thought of not invariably succeeding? How can you ask other poeple to be righteous and not allow themselves to be enslaved by riches, if you do not yourself make this the primary concern of your own life?

Of the Lord, people said – it was a matter of surprise to his hearers – that he spoke with authority. He did not prove what he said, he did not rely on others' authority, not even his Father's; he stated, he read hearts. He stated what he saw in his Father and what he knew about man, about man's inward nature and his destiny. As evangelists, you share in this authoritative teaching by Christ, in so far as you speak as witnesses, and in so far as you express what has genuinely become a living experience for you. We can and must to some degree share in the experience which prompted the Apostle John to say, '*What we have heard, what our own eyes have seen, what we have watched and what our hands have touched of the Word of Life: that we proclaim to you.*'[45] Yes, and we too, by light of faith and experience of love, must have touched Christ, heard Christ, seen Christ. And this experience will give our words the weight of living witness, the force of an experience which we pass on to our friend, a secure assurance lodged in the recesses of the heart, which we feel impelled to share with others.

The mission also requires you to have a vision of men and things corresponding to Christ's own vision of the same. Otherwise, we may lose sight of what evangelism's scope and purpose is. When Brother Charles said that he was duty bound '*to see a soul for the saving in every man*', he was stating a profound truth, if in terms no longer in fashion today. In each man we must see God's creature, a being loved by him as much as he loves us, and we must be so conscious of this that we cannot but desire for our brother what we might desire for ourselves. In him we ought to contemplate the infinite dignity investing him as a person destined to an eternal future. This vision of man should be ever in our minds – whenever we meet a human being to whom we ought to show respect and love. I do not imagine that there can be a single person in the world who would not hope to be treated like this and be the freer for it. Contemplation should help you to develop love for others into a habit of mind, until it becomes a spontaneous and automatic response to your fellow-men. This attitude of mind is an acquired one, as are all other habits.

Yes, we have to contemplate this human-divine fact and see the Kingdom as something in process of achievement, advancing towards God's eternity. I use the word contemplate for brevity when talking of a state of soul resulting from a whole gamut of knowledge, meditation, experience of human nature,

protracted prayer and insights bestowed by the Holy Spirit.
To be lively and fruitful in you, this vision of man must be
maintained and become habitual. Its fruit will then be an infinitely respectful and compassionate love for every human
creature. Such should be the evangelist's attitude, his state of
soul, his convictions, be the actual activities by which his mission is discharged what they may.

You must equip yourselves for witnessing to that by which
you live: for conversing with people, for enlightening them. In
the things of God, there is a wisdom and a knowledge which
are not only the fruits of contemplation, for contemplation
itself postulates a degree of knowledge acquired by study and
meditation. The illuminating action of the Holy Spirit cannot
replace the understanding of the faith acquired by our own
efforts, nor can it make it otiose.

Such are the main requirements for the evangelist's mission.
It goes without saying that the mission forms part of the wider
mission of the Church; if not, it is not likely to be genuine. You
have been sent as members of the Church to proclaim Jesus
Christ to men. And of the Church's faith we have already
spoken, as also of the imperfect quality of its outward witness.
We shall have to come back to this since it deeply concerns us,
we as Christians and religious being so to speak members of
the Church twice over.

We must be convinced of the living unity of the Church. There
can only be one Church, since the Body of Christ is unique.
Offended by the behaviour of some bishops, some priests,
some religious and even of the Vatican, people may tend to distinguish between as it were two Churches. On the one hand,
there is what they call the official or institutional Church. On
the other, the spiritual, evangelical Church, made up of communities of Christians who claim – God alone sounds the
depths of their hearts. – to live, under the impulsion of the
Spirit, a life in true conformity to the Gospel and so be authentic witnesses of Christ's Church, side by side with the official
Church, or in contrast to it.

Out of sympathy for the very poor, out of understanding for
those people who are shocked by the behaviour of part of the
Church's personnel, do we not also run the risk of giving in to
this temptation? Doesn't it sometimes happen that we slip

into using the expression, 'institutional' or 'official Church'? What do we mean? There is no official Church. There is Jesus Christ's Church enfolding, indissolubly united, the whole body of Christians, the Pope himself and the bishops being just as much members of it as any other baptised person, you and me included. In spite of the diversity of function, each is inseparable from the other; all are quickened by the same Spirit. Inevitably some people give scandal or bear counter-witness, as much among the so-called personnel of the Church as among the laity. For the Church is a social entity, disfigured by human failings. I am not talking now about the invisible Kingdom of God, the hidden frontiers of which, as I have already pointed out, run through the indvidual human heart and exceed the body of the Church. But it was to serve that Kingdom *'which is not of this world'* that Jesus founded a Church which could not be other than affected by earthly conditions. You cannot separate yourselves from the Church: not even if belonging to it is humiliating sometimes, or even painful. Who will throw the first stone at the Church? Criticise her openly and ruthlessly, join the chorus of those continually carping at the Church and sometimes even turning her to ridicule? You only wound yourselves: you cannot manage without her nor can you separate yourselves from what will always be the Church of Christ on earth. No other entity, no other spontaneous community of Christians can replace her. One might well ask what Christians have to gain, once their confidence in the Church's leaders has been sapped on the pretext that these leaders' behaviour deserves all the criticism it gets. They risk the weakening of their faith in Christ, the loss of that fulness of light which the Church alone can confer. How can people who treat their brothers, their fellow-members of Christ, with remorseless severity, still exemplify Gospel humility? We must all take care, while witnessing to Gospel ideals, not to sow strife in people's consciences, not to implant seeds of disunity in the hearts of our fellow-Christians.

There are no such things as an official Church and an evangelical Church, with the latter in contrast to the former poor and not institutionalised. This is not the place to go deeply into this, but I had to mention it to give you some inkling of the practical, sometimes painful, problems which you will have to solve. It would be a mistake to imagine that, by virtue of having been called to the Fraternity, you would avoid the serious difficulties which the so-called official Church has not yet succeeded in overcoming. Of which there is one, which we shall all encounter: I mean the extreme difficulty encountered by anyone called to bear comprehensive witness to Jesus Christ in the modern world. The kernel of the Gospel message is the proclamation of eternal life, which people are little disposed to believe in and which rarely even arouses their interest.

The Church is not always well placed for the very reason that it is weighed down by many centuries. Alone of all the societies and institutions of the past, the Church has survived through the ages without ceasing to be herself, earth-shaking political and cultural revolutions notwithstanding; her own internal crises too. She is the only institution the essence of whose message can never be revised or modified. Steadfastness of this type is by no means easy. The deposit entrusted to her is not hers to change. Thus, for example, when the Church persists in affirming the indissolubility of marriage and the sanctity of human life, and in upholding, in opposition to a point of view becoming more and more entrenched and widely held, certain moral values affecting human love, she is accused of being indifferent to contemporary problems and of defending out-dated ethical positions. Now, if the Church judges that certain of her attitudes cannot be subject to revision, this is because she considers that these form part of the deposit entrusted to her by God. She has no power to change them. Why hold the Church to blame? Christianity itself should be arraigned. For the fact is that God has revealed what he intends man and man's behaviour to be. So, to contest this is really contesting the fact that man's duty is to obey God. Of course, in the ways in which she is faithful to her mission, the Church can be clumsy, narrow-minded, and can get trapped in equivocal political situations. And here we are, back at the human condition, which influences the Church as she discharges even the most essential and exalted aspects of her trust!

We are sometimes inclined to consider the Church without reference to God. How many people truly and honestly today believe in a personal, loving God? The Church is still accepted as a spiritual force not to be ignored, on condition that she puts herself at the service of mankind. She is asked to make the preoccupations and problems of the modern world her own and to adapt herself to the purpose. This is complicated. The Church's task is by no means easy. And all the less so since, to express the truths of religion, it is hard to find a language which can be understood by our contemporaries and yet will not be false to the truths which we are trying to convey. Those people particularly who have the supreme responsibility of preserving the Word and deposit of faith have constantly to consider whether what is being contested, the truths or the values under attack, is in fact a part of the deposit entrusted by Christ to the Church, or whether the Church as such has the power to alter them.[46] In circumstances of this sort, the Church particularly needs the Holy Spirit's help. For the Church is Christ; the Church is not the men who compose her and would be free to adapt a message which was theirs: the message is Christ's! Agreed, it has been entrusted to the responsibility of men, who have continually to seek out its deeper meanings, to understand it better and sometimes to make a distinction between what is relative and what is absolute, between what is temporary and what eternal. In obeying the Church, we form part of the leavening action of the Gospel, not to be arrested until the world itself comes to an end. Our participation also extends back to the generations of the past, since spiritual genius and holiness have no age. The holiness preached by the Church, the holiness of the Apostles, of the Desert Fathers, of St Augustine, of St John Chrysostom, of all the great saints of the Church, is always basically the same, in the sense that man is always man, whatever changes may occur in his social or cultural environment. Spiritual genius does not depend on scientific progress; the deepest insights into existence and the meaning of life occur at a different level from that at which the exact or so-called experimental sciences produce results. I have already alluded to this in connexion with our reflections on the nature of man and human destiny. The Church cannot grow old while witnessing to these insights and the knowledge and wisdom accruing from them. To be sure, the language may get out of date, for this is only an outward mode of expression which well may bear the mark of passing time; but not the essential insights and wisdom accumulated in the memory of the Church and mankind. Can we honestly claim that scientific progress and the present state of the world, politics included, make human holiness – or to put it another way, the full flowering of human nature – any easier or harder to achieve? Be man's earthly situation what it may, he will always face the challenge to be holy, as Christ suggests and requires that he should be.

If we consider the moral demands of Christian holiness, we may indeed say that progress perhaps makes this holiness more difficult and complicated to achieve, but also more necessary than ever. For as it gets harder to be truly human, so it gets harder to be a Christian and to be holy, since a holy person is first and foremost a human being. There is no such thing as non-human holiness, nor holiness with unbalanced, or multilated, or as yet not properly balanced, human nature. I am not expressing an opinion on the salvation, in the hope and compassion of God, of all those people living in inhuman conditions through no fault of their own. But the holiness to which Christ's disciples are summoned is an ideal after which we must never cease to strive. The conditions for achieving it coincide exactly with what human commonsense declares to be a 'humane environment', which is what in fact everybody wants.

In certain aspects of morality and society, the Church may easily seem to be lagging behind. The demands of Christian morality take some time to adapt to new situations. And evangelists, more than other people, being in direct contact with the problems and moral situations caused by living conditions in the modern world, are sharply aware of this time-lag. But we are all responsible for it. Each of us has received his task in the Christian community: the theologian has his, the pastors of the Church have theirs. They cannot do everything, and we all need each other. We cannot manage without the supreme pastor's teaching, or without the pastoral foresight of our bishops, anymore than they can do without our humble experience of the daily life of the poor or the witness that we ought to be giving in our vocation and the spiritual experience accruing from that.

This said, how should we react to those people in the

Church, particularly those in positions of responsibility, who bear a counter-witness? This expression means that their behaviour runs counter to the witness which the Church ought to be giving: which witness is a sign among men and, more than that, the *sacrament* of Christ's presence in his Kingdom. Now, a counter-witness tends to distort this sign, to weaken it, locally at least. On the strength of these counter-signs, there are people who assert that the Church is no longer bearing witness to the Gospel, that she is on the side of the exploiter, that she is the prisoner of an out-dated system or political outlook, that she apparently accords direct or indirect approval to a type of society based on the profit motive, that she does not share the aspirations of the poor, that she is not sufficiently worried about injustice. Such a judgment may be over-simplified, and may also be too sweeping to be accurate. Nonetheless, it is a fact that the Church's position and historic role in some countries has lent support to those who criticise her on these grounds. Be that as it may, this should lead us to examine the kind of relationship existing between the Church's evangelistic mission and what we call politics: the political dimension of human activities. Let us be clear at the outset that we shall be concentrating exclusively on problems raised by the peculiar situation and vocation of the Fraternity itself. But first of all we ought to listen to what the Church has to say about herself and about the way she performs her evangelistic mission in the world; and this we shall find in the documents of the Council. You will find more teaching on this subject in *Gaudium et spes, Lumen gentium* and other important conciliar documents than you might expect. You ought to ponder, assimilate and refer to them for light on your course. Do not expect the Holy Spirit to give you personal guidance and suggest what you ought to believe or do in a sphere where he has already given his judgment through the *magisterium* of his Church. The Spirit will be acting in us – of this be sure – but through or starting with what he has said to the Church. Christ said of those who expected a personal sign before being converted, '*They have Moses and the Prophets, let them listen to them! . . . If they will not listen either to Moses or to the prophets, they will not be convinced, even if someone were to rise from the dead.*'[7] For us, Moses and the prophets mean the Church as well. Are we to behave like Lazarus's brothers in the parable?

We wait for a personal revelation, something new; we claim to have discovered the Gospel afresh. I reply: listen first to the prophets, listen to your Church! It may be you have not been listening properly, have not been putting the right question to her, have not really grasped what she has already said about her mission. And hence, you have not given the matter enough thought, have not sufficiently assimilated what she says, to be able to evaluate a new situation in the light of her teaching.

Every Christian is in the Church, and in so far as he is commissioned by the Church to evangelise – as we have been twice over by virtue of our religious consecration – the Church's envoy is totally dependent on the Church. We are talking about a mission which, as we have already seen, absorbs our entire life. Being an evangelist is a life-long state for anyone specially chosen by God for this mission; whereas the laity at large discharge this mission through their family, professional, civic and political activities. The situation of the Christian layman, even when high-mindedly and totally committed to the apostolate on a personal basis, is different from that of the person whose vocation it is to be commissioned by the Church to evangelise. I repeat this because people often tend to minimise the idea of mission. Whichever way the mission is to be performed, the person called by God ought to be aware of this responsibility of life-long commitment. The hand of God is on him. Read the accounts of the calling of Elijah and Jeremiah once again.[48] '*Woe to me, if I do not proclaim the Gospel!*' St Paul was to write to the Corinthians.[49]

But this will not be the first time we have thought about all this. It is not idle or speculative to ask what distinguishes the mission of the Christian layman in the world from the mission of someone commissioned by the Church to proclaim the Gospel: for it is important for us to acquire an evangelist's mentality; on this will depend the way our actions are orientated and the choices which we shall have to make, political ones most of all.

The Church has always professed herself to be outside politics and, in a wider sense, unconcerned with temporal affairs. Even so, she has certainly interfered in politics over the centuries. What are we to think about that? What is the situation now? Attentive reading of conciliar documents touching on

this topic gives us a clearer view of the Church's role in this very delicate and increasingly important field.
First of all, we must define what we mean by politics. This can mean a complex body of sciences and facts which dictate the choice of a political philosophy, an ideology and an economic system with a view to producing effective action, be it for the setting up of new institutions, or for the acquiring of power, or for the transforming of society – as by action through trade unions to implement specific claims – or even for preparing the ground for a complete revolution. Understood in this sense, politics postulates skills and the sacrifice of time and energy on a scale excluding any alternative mission. *'You cannot serve two masters at once.'* [50] I say this, not speaking from an eschatological point of view – which would take us out of the sphere of political activity – but comparing two types of human activity, each of them demanding to be the dominant factor in a person's life. Take a doctor, for instance, who in the practice of his profession spends all day looking after the sick and keeping his medical knowledge up to date: he cannot be a political leader as well, or even a political activist. He has to choose between medicine and politics, or risk practising neither of them properly. Activities of the political or evangelistic type have far too serious effects on human destiny for them to be performed incompetently. Respect and love for human beings forbid. Incompetence in such matters can have dire effects, leading to further injustice and an aggravation of human hardships and suffering. This is true of the doctor unable to concentrate on his patient's welfare, and it is true of the politician too. In this sense, then, politics do not fall within the competence of the Church.

The advent and revelation of Christ in human history modified nothing and revealed nothing new in the political sphere; the conditions for creating true democracy or the laws regulating the economy are still the same. One might go so far as to say that the coming of the industrial age and technological progress have done more to upset the political order and our political outlook than the proclamation of the Gospel ever did. To Christians who wonder what their specific role in the political sphere should be, I reply that, in the political sphere itself, nothing distinguishes them from other citizens. The same conclusion has eventually been reached, after much trial and error, by certain Catholic Action groups. The complexity of present-day socio-political conditions, the nature and variety of qualifications needed to promote a progressive policy, all contribute to show that the specific role of the Christian is not to be found here. Yet, by affirming that she stands outside these political options, the Church surely gives the impression of siding too easily with the injustices associated with the established order? By standing outside the political debate, the Church may consequently seem to be partisan. By keeping silent, may she not seem to be supporting the political order? And this encourages us to ask if the word politics may not have another meaning, denoting a sphere in which the Church is and should insist that she is competent to speak.

In a more general sense, politics also denotes all that concerns the whole complex of social relationships in the organism of the human city. Now, these human, social and political relationships are subject to the obligations of the Divine Law and to those of Christ's law of love. The Gospel leaven, that is the Christians in the city, must incessantly incite people to be concerned for greater justice, respect for the poor, concern for the rights of the weak, of the aged, of strangers, and be vigilant over safeguarding essential liberties. The defence and fostering of all those *'sacred rights of the individual'* to use Paul VI's own words, is the Church's mission in the world. Hence, it is one of the Church's duties to foster the ideal of man as follower of Christ and to denounce, oppose and condemn whatever may be contrary to this ideal. The Church should do this by trying to make her witness effective. Through her members, whether laymen, religious or bishops, this is the way the Church fulfils her prophetic mission.

For it is the prophet's mission to make God's voice heard in human affairs and to proclaim how God requires men to behave as social beings. The Church performs this task particularly through the voice of those whom she deputes to be evangelists. And in so doing, she is the voice of mankind's conscience, making itself heard through those whom she has deputed for the purpose. The Bible shows us that the prophets were the preservers of the Covenant, not as regards the liturgy nor the study of and commenting on the Law – for these were the jobs of the priests, scribes and doctors of the Law – but as regards the concrete demands of that Law as they affected the behaviour of the individual, of social classes, or of the entire nation, in their loyalty to their covenantal obligations. The history of the Old Covenant shows us that the prophet did not have an easy mission, Impelled by the Spirit, he had to perform it in spite of himself and even at risk of his life. We have not properly realised that this mission has now devolved on the Church and on those sent to evangelise the world in the Church's name. They cannot escape this gruelling aspect of their mission, since it is part and parcel of the task.

Thus, the prophet does not deliver the principles of the Law in general or theoretical terms; this is not his job. Faced with concrete individual situations, faced with a specific event, he publicly proclaims what the Divine Law requires. St John the Baptist, the prophet sent to prepare the way for the coming of the Kingdom, was not content to utter generalities. His courage in denouncing concrete evils, in boldly condemning King Herod's conduct – '*It is against the Law to take your brother's wife,*'[51] – cost him his life.

Ever since the Gospel was first proclaimed, this mission has been uninterruptedly exercised in the Church by bishops, apostles, men and women raised by the Holy Spirit. We know how freely St John Chrysostom used to speak. Unafraid to contradict the Emperor to his face, he was exiled for his pains. And in our own times, we have plenty of other examples. All those bishops, for instance, who – be the risks they incur what they may – unhesitatingly spring to the defence of the poor and oppressed and proclaim the concrete demands of the Gospel, in contradiction to those of the civil power. This is why the silence of some Churches at crying injustices and the infringements of human rights looks like a tacit compromise with evil and a betrayal of their mission. Obviously, even in the bosom of the Church, you will – and I can't think why people should be surprised at this! – inevitably encounter human weakness and mediocrity. But for our part, we shall not forget how Brother Charles of Jesus at Béni-Abbès and in the Hoggar, when faced with the evil of slavery and the injustices of the government, never stopped vigorously denouncing them.

I now come to the more concrete problems confronting the Fraternity in the political sphere; those which need to be solved in a way consistent with our vocation. It seems timely to talk about this now that you are about to commit yourselves and are aware of the contemplative dimension of your mission as evangelists. If you are consecrated in the Church to the task of evangelisation, you have your share in the Church's prophetic mission. You are to exercise this in a particular way, appropriate to the society and people whose earthly lot you share, since the essential thing about the Fraternity's vocation is this sharing of the lot of a given class or of a given environment. And this is all the truer, I repeat, because the prophet's mission is not to preach in the abstract but to insert the leaven of the Gospel into the heart of human situations. Whereas the mission of theologian or Biblical scholar is to research into and teach the content of the divine message, the prophet for his part has to try and translate the requirements of that message into action and see that they are effectively put into practice.

The evangelist's task requires him to be ready to react against all the powers of evil at work in the world. The prophet must have the gift of discernment, to detect the frequently hidden activities of these powers. People must feel that we, because we belong to Christ, are clearly and painfully aware of this evil. And the awareness will be painful because, like Christ and with him, we have to take the burden on ourselves of all the sufferings of unhappy men, of the poor, of those enduring injustice, of all those crushed by life, of all those who are the worn out and despairing victims of an uncaring society. This is how we really become sharers in the mystery of Christ Crucified. Jesus was the Suffering Servant, the man crushed by scorn and pain, whom the Prophet Isaiah displays to us as bowed down by our diseases and pierced because of our transgressions.[52] Thus he reveals the mysterious bond which links Christ's sufferings to those of the poor. And here of course he means all human hardships, all those that make a human being, thus humbled, open his heart to the gentleness and compassion coming to him from the One who alone can heal the wounds inflicted by evil. This is the sense in which the Bible speaks of the poor, not in that of a self-aware social class as identified by ideological analysis at a given moment in history. In God's eyes, the poor are a spiritual family, not a sociological phenomenon, even though these two concepts of poverty may to some degree be related.

In the Bible, the poor constitute a spiritual family, for which God feels a special and virtually exclusive preference. What the poor have in common is their lack of the earthly goods which confer power; and hence they are usually the victims of injustice and of other people's sins. Thus oppressed by evil, they, more than others, embody the need for liberation, which Christ came to achieve. In the accomplishing of this immense task, there is a connexion, indeed an inter-dependence, between the liberation from sin which Christ alone can bring, and the efforts which men themselves must make to liberate society from the servitude and oppression which in its varying forms is caused by sin. For it is true to say that the sufferings inflicted on people by others – war, economic enslavement, unjust institutions, the primacy of profit, the suppression of liberty – are the effects of sin. And indeed, though acting in good-faith and only seeking the good of their fellow-men, people are, whether directly or indirectly, in spite of themselves, more or less responsible for these sufferings and enslavements, since their human limitations entail a lack of knowledge and appreciation of situations. Now, these limitations, often producing tragic results at the collective level, are the in-eradicable trace in us of the primordial fall of man. In the awareness, which you must safeguard, of your evangelistic mission, you must not lose sight of the quest for human solutions to questions raised by the existence of evil in the world, of evil often institutionalised, when economic con-siderations become more important than the paramount claims of human dignity.

In performing this prophetic mission in the name of Gospel and Church, and in the service of the people among whom you are living, the Gospel's claims are to be the ideal by which you orientate people's efforts towards a better life and better socie-ty. The evangelist cannot refuse to be the guide, the adviser, the voice of conscience, the instigator to action, the reprover, the trainer of other people's consciences. These activities are part of his evangelistic mission, most particularly when they are geared to concrete situations and immediate problems.

You will not normally be required to make an 'ideological' choice. I use the word 'ideological' as short-hand for everything bearing on the choice of the economic or political means to be adopted in combatting injustice, oppression and whatever other evils may apply. It is not within the evangelist's competence to intervene in this sphere which involves a different kind of commitment, itself tending to absorb all one's energies and indeed deserving an equally total commitment. I said: normally. Of course, a complex situation may occasionally arise, in which the evangelist is obliged to make some sort of social or political decision.

All this must sound obvious to a man of faith, aflame with love for his fellow-men. I must confess, I do not see any need to devise a new theology to show that love can and should have a political dimension. Aren't the claims of the Law of Love enough in themselves? If I love men, how can I bear to see them suffering, without feeling obliged to intervene and act on the causes making them suffer? If I love men, how can I bear them to be prisoners to a degrading slavery, without trying to deliver them from it? If I love the poor, how can I bear them to be the victims of unjust, oppressive systems, without feeling obliged to change those institutions? I do not need any other reason for taking action. This seems enough to me: for reflection on the political means of liberation is not within the province of theology. If I truly understand Christ's teaching in the Gospel, if I allow myself to accept the claims of Truth about the dignity of man as the image of God, if in self-renunciation I consent to obey the claims of love and justice, regardless of what these cost me, why should I need a new theological interpretation of Christ's message?

When I consider how Christ behaved to men, as the Gospel records this, I find that he spoke up boldly to all: from which I realise that I choose a difficult path when following him. Jesus's relationships with men took place at a level transcending all considerations of social class, transcending and often controverting the judgments based on outward behaviour which men commonly pass on one another. This is why Jesus often shocked and scandalised those who knew him, not only by welcoming sinners and prostitutes, but also by frequenting the wealthy, even those belonging to the tax-collecting class, which had grown rich at the people's expense and was accordingly detested. As people consecrated to evangelism, we bear this same important obligation. When continuing Christ's mission and called by him to proclaim every facet of his Gospel, we cannot adopt another point of view from his in dealing with our fellow-men. Destined by vocation to be evangelists to the poor, it is not only lawful but our bounden duty to share the preoccupations, all the attempts and all the efforts, of the poor to liberate themselves. But while doing this, we must not forget that at the level of Christ's presence in mankind and that of the Kindom of God, we have to rise above all consideration of division, class, race and nationality.

We must not forget either that Jesus always refused to become involved in anything to do with the political liberation of his people or to meddle in temporal affairs. The Gospel makes it plain that attempts were made on several occasions to trap him, by encouraging him to compromise himself over the Roman occupation of Palestine, or to assume the sort of messianic role which all Israel was eagerly awaiting. When asked one day to solve a legal case over rights of succession, Jesus gave a twofold answer. First, he refused to become embroiled in the matter. '*Who appointed me your judge, or the arbitrator of your claims?*'[53] His second answer was to warn against the false scale of values inherent in wealth. And he told them the parable of the rich farmer who built an extension to his granaries.[54] And ended thus, '*This is what happens when a man stores up treasure for himself, instead of becoming rich in the eyes of God.*' Jesus was on earth to evangelise, not to assure a more just distribution of worldly goods. We must never lose sight of Christ's attitude to this. There will always be something in the evangelist's mission which cannot be absorbed or totally expressed by undertakings, decisions and positions taken over social injustices and particular situations. Nothing is as simple as it looks!

But should we go further? I have already mentioned the possibility of exceptional situations arising. Could there be urgent cases when you would be called, as people consecrated to the Gospel, to take part in some kind of political activity involving direct action, to become involved in behaviour implying some sort of ideological alignment on your part, even if only temporary? The case which often occurs is a struggle between unions and management, since the aspirations of the poor are principally expressed through trade unions in the industrially developed countries, as providing the means for achieving their freedom. Organised and effective action of this sort not only corresponds to the aspirations of, but is a necessity for, the poor in their normal course of development : from the days of Leo XIII onwards the Church has continually emphasised that trade unionism was a duty for the working man. For the poor and oppressed, it is a *sine qua non* of their dignity as men, the aim of the unions being to acquire that moral freedom to which all men should aspire and which in turn presupposes decent living conditions. Surely respect for the poorest and love for all men, inspired by Christianity, should make it our duty to collaborate in improving the lot of those less privileged?

Or again, urgent situations may arise, in which we are the only people equipped to take effective action. The evangelist's consecration to works of love, truth and justice then leaves us no choice. When I meet someone sick and deserted, don't I naturally have to try and help him? If I find myself near a drowning man, don't I at least have to try and rescue him? Similarly then, if in the society where I am living, there are people enduring slavery, don't I have to do everything I can to set them free? This question surely provides an easy answer?

In this sphere and particularly in the case of slavery, we have the example of Brother Charles to guide us. He never hesitated to denounce that abuse severely, to condemn the compromises of the government and to do everything he could to abolish such a state of affairs. You know too how later with the Touareg he took a continuous interest in all their problems, making it his concern to put an end to injustice of every sort. He used to advise the chiefs responsible and even suggest what decisions they ought to take. His letters to General Laperrine are of great interest on this subject. Yet he was always most careful not to replace established authority by his own.[55]

In the history of our Fraternity, I might draw your attention to an example which you perhaps know about already, of this type of temporal involvement as exerting an exceptional claim on our mission. I mean the Fraternity at X – where, faced with the urgent and dramatic situation of a defenceless populace in peril of being deprived of the land indispensable for its survival, the Brothers took the immediate initiative of founding a co-operative as the only effective way of solving the problem. The assumption of this type of responsibility was neither within their terms of reference nor within their qualifications as evangelists, the forming of so important a co-operative as this being a very complicated matter indeed. But given the circumstances, there was no time to be lost. I ratified the Brothers' decisions, asking them to find a competent lay manager as quickly as they could and to prepare the people themselves gradually to assume responsibility for this collective activity. A few months later, the Brothers had nothing more to do with running the co-operative.

It may be, one day, you will be confronted with a similar situation. Make a point then of taking level-headed decisions, bearing in mind what your essential and original mission is. Even when you are obliged to take the initiative, you must still be absolutely convinced that the distinction between the evangelistic mission and socio-political action is not a mere form of words. Between the vocation of the militant Christian trade unionist and that of the evangelist and prophet, there is an essential distinction – and by no means a trivial one, since on it depends the aim and effectiveness of either of these two types of activity. Not to give true weight to the distinction would lead the Church into abandoning her specific mission; for this would soon be absorbed and transposed into a sort of temporal messianism in search of an ideology capable of putting it into political effect – a role which Christianity in the true sense, i.e. of religious fidelity to a revealed message, is not designed to fulfil.

This is neither an imaginary problem nor a theoretical distinction. You have only to consult your own experience and think of what is going on in other countries. When, over and above earning his keep, a brother becomes so involved in trade union activity that he becomes an activist and organiser, isn't it inevitable that his commitment to this will become the ruling concern of his life and that he will devote every free moment to it? Now, religious life requires that our time be consecrated to God; inevitably, however, a brother so heavily committed to political activity will be bound to devote less and less time to prayer, until he eventually stops praying

altogether. Theological and Biblical studies will be replaced
by books on political and ideological topics, since he will feel
he needs to read these to guide his own course of action or to
train other activists like himself. It is hard to imagine that his
relationships with other people will not be profoundly altered,
since his commitment will inevitably affect his choice of ac-
quaintances and what he and they talk and think about. I
don't see how this can be avoided, since we are discussing jobs
all-absorbing in themselves and impossible to pursue by
half-measures. Hence, the witness he gives will be affected. If I
am no longer a man of prayer, but merely would like to be one
– and intention is not enough – if people no longer see me
pray, the witness of my life is affected. If my ruling concern is
no longer Christ's essential mission of revealing eternal life –
the just relationships to be established between men being
only one effect of the Kingdom of God – I can no longer maintain the proper perspectives of my vocation as evangelist: eternal life and the supreme liberation of man in the mystery of
Christ.

   I agree, it is hard to draw the line between these two attitudes at the level of the activities themselves, since a man's
life cannot be divided into different compartments. Nor can
evangelisation be reduced to exclusive and specific activities,
such as the literal proclamation of the Gospel and religious instruction. The evangelist lives and acts as a witness to Christ.
Now, this witness is not only expressed in all sorts of different
attitudes and works, but has to be given in very complex
human situations. I also have to allow for the slowness and
unpredictability with which the Kingdom of God makes progress in others; which progress it is the evangelist's task to
stimulate, encourage, respect and strengthen turn by turn. It
may be I have to wait for years before being able to mention
Christ's name to the people around me. Evangelisation cannot
be planned in advance; it can only be entrusted to the wisdom,
devotion and free judgment of the messenger. We cannot solve
the question of how to evangelise by arbitarily simplifying it,
sometimes for reasons of personal conviction, or of timidity, or
of preference for one person rather than another. In discharging your responsibilites as evangelists, each of you will have a
different approach, depending on your disposition, your
character and the contemplative dimension of your life.

Different brothers will act differently in a given situation. There is no single answer to the question, nor a single method to adopt.

A notion about the evangelistic vocation held by some of the Protestant Churches used to lay an absolute obligation on the apostle literally to proclaim the coming of Christ in all places, *in season and out of season*, regardless of the results, if any. Until the proclamation had been made, the missionary's conscience remained burdened by responsibility for the souls of those to whom he had not preached. The proclamation once made, whether by the spoken or the written word, freed the missionary's conscience of its burden.[56] I shall give you two typical examples of this sense of evangelistic responsibility carried to the extreme, and indeed reminiscent of the way in which the prophets of old were, as it were, constrained to perform their mission by the Spirit of God. In northern India, on the Sikkim frontier, I happened to be one day in a Tibetan market where caravans formed up before leaving for Lhassa. I was the only European there and was very interested in the crowds of Tibetans and what they were doing, when I suddenly noticed a European couple ensconced on a mat. The lady crouching on the ground and the man standing up, they were proclaiming the Gospel in Tibetan, without bothering to notice whether anyone was listening and without taking any preparatory measures to interest their potential audience. Without any sign of fear, they were proclaiming Jesus Christ in the middle of the crowd, who barely seemed aware that they were there. People walked by, looked at them, paused a moment out of curiosity: that was all. I was impressed by their courage, thinking that I would never have dared to behave like that and finding a thousand good reasons for not doing so!

On another occasion I was in Kabyle and the White Fathers told me something very similar. A Protestant clergyman visited them and asked them to show him where he could find a fair sized gathering of people. One of the Fathers took him to the Moorish coffee-shop in the village, where the Kabyle men met to pass the time of day while playing dominoes and drinking coffee. As soon as he got inside, the clergyman drew himself up and began to speak, 'Please listen to me for a moment. Would you mind being quiet for a few minutes.' All the Moslems raised their heads in surprise; silence fell. In a few

words, the clergyman proclaimed salvation in Jesus Christ to
these people and then went out again. Somewhat dis-
concerted, the Kabyles resumed their game of dominoes. As
regards the missionary, having now proclaimed Jesus Christ
to these people, he felt no further responsibility for their salvation.

Such proceedings may well make us smile. But I don't know
if there is anyone here who would have had the courage to do
the same. While admiring these ministers' forthright convictions, we should advance a different concept of evangelism,
slow and more cautious in approach, entered upon only after
preliminary soundings have been made and, more particularly, after our potential converts have made up their minds to
listen to us. Yes, of course. But I think that sometimes we are
too sure of being right! Between opposing notions of how the
Gospel ought to be preached – as to its nature, its content and
the way to do it – there are many degrees and nuances.
Wouldn't it be a good thing if, from time to time, we were to
take our incumbent responsibility more seriously? Read the
Acts of the Apostles and St Paul's epistles once again. I often
feel at fault in my passivity – pretty comfortable when all is
said and done – where my mission is concerned!

In each of our fraternities then we have to ask this question:
What should our policy be? Should we be patient or impatient
over proclaiming Christ? Should we make long-term or only
short-term preparation? Should we pause before going ahead?
The unanswerable preliminary question: Are they ready to
have Christ explicitly proclaimed to them? In the nature of
things we have to go on putting this question to ourselves. We
have to keep deepening our awareness of our vocation, and so
draw the practical conclusions appropriate to the environment
or to the region. Let us be honest and clear-headed enough to
recognise the true motivation behind our attitudes: some of us
are timid, others more active and urgent; some will pin their
faith on the grace that belief in Jesus Christ and his coming
automatically confer, others will consider socio-political
liberation as the first prerequisite for any advance. Let no one
claim to be exclusively right in a matter so essential for us and
above all for the people to whom we have been sent! Let us be
sure that our own faith is robust and open-hearted. Let us

draw light from the Church, by which to renew our sense of evangelistic vocation. Let us feel, as the Apostle Paul felt, impelled to preach Jesus Christ, not waiting for the moment, for that will never come, when all conditions favourably concur. Should we have had the courage to talk about the resurrection of the dead on the Agora in Athens to such rationalistic people as the Athenians? The Apostle was prompted by the Spirit and acted in obedience to his love for Christ. Whereas today every evangelistic mission is conditioned by all sorts of organised and co-ordinated activities, subject to a host of preliminaries concerned with development and so forth.

The Fraternity is responsible for a specific evangelistic task, and this must reflect our specific vocation, although we cannot precisely lay down the means and methods which ought to be adopted. It is up to the individual to see what this task is and to be faithful to it; and you cannot be faithful to it, if you are not aware of Christ's presence within you. We have already explained the conditions and consequences of this awareness, of this basic attitude. Passing then to action, having decided on the methods to be used, you have to proceed with commonsense, not make rash judgments and not behave as a clique. For we are not the only evangelists in the world: we must co-operate with the other ones, in union with the local Church. Above all, take account of the fact that committing yourself to the type of activity which can result in your becoming a political or trade union activist is full of risk. I say it again: the ruling concern of your life and the witness it is to give are those of a disciple of Christ. You belong to him. This conviction should be with you always and should be forcefully expressed in your attitudes and actions, even if it runs counter to the prevailing mentality of your environment. People must know that you belong to Christ. You must also keep your sense of the relative nature of political solutions as a means to human liberation. Convictions make people effective. But dogmatically imposing – as the only possible way – an ideology, itself relative, would be doing positive harm. You must not countenance this approach. People who think they have the ideal and unique solution for human progress end up by believing that they have a duty to impose it by political and ideological force.[57]

Let your minds and hearts remain attuned to the Gospel message. Meditating on the Gospel of St John, you cannot fail to take note of what he says about the forces opposed to the Kingdom of God: about a world dominated by the organised powers of evil, by the worship of money and the exclusive quest for profit with a view to promoting exclusively economic growth. These powers, whether occult or overt, governing the world and oppressing human kind, wear different faces and bear different names: you may call them imperialism, capitalism, neo-colonialism, fascism, ideological totalitarianism, and, not to strain at a gnat, any economic or political system infringing the sacred rights and essential liberties of the individual. The *world* with which Christ contrasted his Kingdom is as though inspired by evil. You must yourselves maintain that clear, enlightened, contemplative gaze that Jesus turned on the world – an all-embracing gaze which will prevent you from falling under its spell. For, if you did, you would no longer be attuned to the message which Jesus has entrusted you with. Wherever you are, however you are placed, however much involved you are with people struggling for justice and peace, never let this contemplative gaze grow dim, nor let the eternal force of the Gospel fade. Be concerned with the poorest of mankind. And let the poor, for you as for Christ, be those who plumb the depths of human suffering, the infirm, the sick, the deserted, the despairing, the dying; you would not still be Christ's representatives if you did not make it your job to care for them. Even when you are involved with people collectively organised to improve their lot, do not forget that near these activists, in the same district, in the same village, there are men dying, women deserted, people mourning, weeping and despairing. Christ's place is there, among these poor people, and hence his messengers' place is with them too: and that means you. If you were to lose your sense of involvement in human suffering in its acutest form, and of your involvement with people confronted by death, you would lose your sense of Christ. To sum up, I say once again that your principal landmark and the only solution to your personal difficulties in a life consecrated to proclaiming the Gospel lies in your constantly contemplating the mystery of Christ: and this cannot be done unless you devote time to prayer. This is obvious, exacting, vital.

If you were now to ask me how you should direct your lives, I should simply say this: You are witnesses of Jesus Christ; this makes immense demands on your liberty and courage, and requires you to have that same vision of the world and human destiny as Christ had. You will be his witnesses to people whom you will serve and whose lot you will share. And that is where, you will resolve – not somewhere else – you will have to live that mission with its prophetic demands, humbly applying it in practical terms to those people's daily lives. And while it is true that you are called to share their aspirations and even some of their struggles, you will only ever do this as their apostle, their consecrated brother, their Gospel witness. That is why you have been sent to them. If you ceased being all this to them, you would be no use to them at all.

I say no more. In touching on this subject, I am more than aware of having broached matters so vast that I have risked presenting an incomplete picture. How can we express everything about our life in a handful of words? The unknowable, intangible, mysterious dimension of creatures encompasses us on every side. Let us live in the humble practicalities of the here-now. But amid the complexity of things and schools of thought, we must nonetheless have firm, clear, solid landmarks. And these you will find in your faith, in the Church, in your Fraternity, provided always that you do not stop being a contemplative. I have said this before! But the Church and the Fraternity themselves in their truest reality can only be apprehended by faith. By no other means can you carry out your vocation and still be able to be witnesses and prophets of God. Your Fraternity would then be no more than a team of like-minded, active friends. You have to serve people in the truth – and must believe that there is one! – in the quest for their highest good, constantly concerned to proclaim Jesus Christ to the people to whom you have been sent by him.

VIII

Obedience Equals Love, Unity and Service

It remains for me to offer a few reflections on the subject of obedience in religious life.

In Jesus, we have already considered that fundamental attitude leading him to live literally in a state of obedience to his Father. While Jesus sat, tired, on the margin of Jacob's Well near Samaria, he looked out over the fields of ripening wheat. His disciples had gone to buy food in the village; when they came back and urged him to eat something, he replied, '*I have food to eat which you do not know about . . . My food is to do the will of the One who has sent me and to complete his work.*'[38] This saying of Christ's is very revealing about his inner life. Food is what sustains, what gives growth, what is indispensable. It seems, therefore, that if Jesus was not doing the will of the One who had sent him, he would not have gone on living. Now, without our often being aware of this, the same thing is true of us. We have to eat food which we sometimes find hard to accept, either out of forgetfulness, or carelessness, or downright rejection. We do not know what that food is. Jesus himself said, '*I have food to eat which you do not know about.*' Even his closest apostles did not understand. They had not pierced the secret of the Father's design, so much a part of Christ's life as to be his very reason for existing. In Christ's conception of his Passion and the founding of his Church, he was to be very much alone. No one could ever grasp what he alone could know about his Father's design for him. What he did tell his disciples about this in no way conveyed to them how utterly their Master's freedom, heart and life entire were ruled by the constant habit of obedience to the mysterious and constant will of his Father.

But, you will object, aren't we in a different position from Christ, whose personal lot was unique? Whereas we men of flesh and blood, so totally subject to earthly social conditioning, whose daily task and lot on earth is basically of no interest to anyone except ourselves: how can we know the Father's will, know his design for us, thoroughly enough for us to make it the reason for living and the food of our lives?

Yet, when you commit yourself to embrace the religious life of the Fraternity, deliberately responding to a call from Jesus, aren't you in fact setting out to meet God's design for you, a personal design, his loving reciprocation of your commitment? Your love for the person of Jesus, with its claims, should have absolute primacy over all other preoccupations, because of him who is its object. Now, this is not always perceived as having first claim. All the same, your choice has been made to live for him, your Christ, unreservedly; and because you belong to him, you share with him in carrying out his mission. It is not in fact possible to belong to Jesus without sharing in the depths of his personality, I mean, in his relationship with his Father and in his obedience. You cannot love him without being athirst to obey him in all things. '*Obedience is the yardstick of love*,' wrote Brother Charles. If love between two beings is defined as the faculty of putting oneself in the other's place and of living in him, this ultimately means wanting the same things. When the being whom we love is also our God, we know that his will ought to be the rule of our life and our existence. And thus obedience in a most special sense becomes the yardstick of love.

I am sure many of you too, like Brother Charles, have grasped this identity between love and obedience, have grasped it quite spontaneously under the very impulsion of the Lord's summons and without its entering your head to question the demands this makes of you or to dispute them in the name of reason or of the freedom of the will. Without question, however, does not mean without resistance. Father de Foucauld admits in his letters that what he found most painful as a Trappist was obeying, 'renouncing his judgment' to use his own expression, by which he meant his own way of seeing things. Nevertheless he applied himself wholeheartedly to obeying out of love.

And this leads us to ask a fundamental question about the nature of religious obedience. We must understand the deeper significance of and reason for this obedience, and disregard the somewhat narrow or even deviant forms it took for a number of years before the Council, causing problems from time to time in religious life. This is all the more important since not only do we have to be personally convinced of the function which religious obedience should have in our own lives, but we have a duty to make it acceptable to our contemporaries as well: which is not an easy thing to do in the prevailing state of opinion. For we find ourselves living in times when man is confronted by new and complicated conditions which oblige him to reconsider his own nature and to try and rediscover what he is and what he ought to be by exercise of freedom of choice.

Yet there is another reality: if you look at mankind as a whole, you will see that all men, as soon as they have divided themselves into groups, start giving themselves laws. They are well aware that individually and collectively they need to obey an ideal, some preconception or other of human nature. Some of them will say that they only owe obedience to themselves. The question is then to know whether man ought to obey someone else to fulfil himself as man and achieve his destiny. In the old days, people used to make an ideal of human nature. This had its laws, which could only be broken at the risk of self-destruction. This notion is now under attack: people condemn it as reflecting a static concept of the universe. Man now regards himself as unstable, as involved in the evolutionary process. Therefore he must try to adapt to new situations at each stage of his evolutionary development, affirming that it is for him and him alone to decide what is best for him. Regardless of the merits of this point of view, the fact remains that man goes on, as in the past, obeying some ideal or other. Many people still think in terms of a religious ethic, however clearly or dimly conceived, allowing them to define the ideal man: Moslems, Budhists, Jews, Christians all have religious traditions. Modern ethnology shows how primitive peoples, even small and apparently very backward groups, obey laws, not merely to survive but in order to maintain respect for their dignity as human beings. Others, again, submit to the often very exacting ideal of the new type of human being envisaged by communist ideologists; they are subject to systems of thought which, even when denying any value to metaphysics, are effectively perpetuating the ideas of the religions which they have replaced.[59]

The question then is this: Is the individual the master of his own life, to decide what his own conduct should be at the most intimate, private level of his personal life, without any reference to social behaviour, which latter is the only form of behaviour on which society can act? Alone with himself, what is man? Am I free to make decisions in successive situations in the light of what I think best for me and for others, without reference to a fixed system of values? The more highly organised human societies become, the more insistent becomes what might be called ideological obedience, which requires that the individual behave as the collective interest dictates. Under totalitarian communist governments, ideological obedience is imposed: is no longer a matter of choice. Can this then still be called obedience?[60]

We Christians however believe that man owes obedience to God, who alone really knows what man is and what he ought to be. He alone understands the frailty of the human heart and the extent of human ignorance sufficiently to be able to show the path his creatures ought to follow and the laws they should obey to become truly man. By this obedience, then, man learns to discover the image of God borne within him and to respect it and develop it. This is what we believe. Hence we must know about the forms which this obedience takes, for they are various and many.

As man becomes more and more aware of his position in the universe and cosmos, so he becomes more aware of the exigencies of his situation in universal time, as also in the history already his. For reflective people who believe in God, this means the discovery of a providential plan. Accepting this plan, receiving it as coming from God, is the basis of all obedience. And this obedience consists not only in a wondering discovery of God's general plan but also in trying to understand this design as it very personally affects me; in accepting myself as the living being I am and as my family, my environment and my upbringing have moulded me. Joyfully accepting myself is my initial act of obedience to God's creative design as directly and personally concerned with me.

But we shall have to go further than this, for this obedience to God my Creator, to all-provident God, leads me to obey the laws of my own nature, and then to obey other people: for this,

we must understand, is how love functions. The discovery that
obedience is the yardstick of love not only affects the way my
own plans and wishes conform to God's designs and wishes,
but obedience is also the law of that love which I ought to have
for my fellow-men. Obeying men is an obligatory expression
of love, showing itself in devotion and readiness to serve. Once
our love is expended, not on lifeless things but on beings en-
dowed with freedom, will, brain, seeking what is good for
them, we are committed to one path of obedience – since
thenceforth we have to want with them what is in their best interest and to work with them to attain it.

God's plan however goes further still, and our obedience to
Christ assumes a very different dimension, by becoming
obedience to the Christian vocation. We have seen how faith is
a form of obedience, since it hands over our thoughs and
wishes to Christ as a worthy expression of our confidence in
the dignity and truth of the Son of God. But he is not only
true. He is very Truth, he is also the way, and he is life. In giving myself body and soul to him, I therefore find the path my
life should take; I find a true light to illuminate the way
destined for me. This assurance of coming to the truth affects
my nature and life at the deepest. By entrusting myself to
Christ, I find love's fulfilment. He is my life, my whole life.

As I discover the living Christ, so I have to live out the consequences of this meeting, and these affect a whole gamut of
relationships of which we have already spoken. I have to subordinate my choices, my wishes, my desires, to obeying God –
for except by this, I know, man can never find the norms of
true self-fulfilment.

How is this obedience to be translated into practical terms? It
will have to be done by degrees, for the path is not easy to
follow. We are by nature much more sensitive to the social,
human environment of sense-perceptions than we are to the
divine. The Word of God has to reveal itself to us and
transform us: and this implies continual effort on our part to
meet it halfway, to receive and assimilate it. When Jesus said
that his food was to do the will of the One who had sent him,
he meant us to take note of this word *food*. Receiving the Word
of God involves continual, daily, life-giving nourishment, it is
true; but there must be assimilation too. This food must

transform us and make the image of God grow within us. In the Psalms and other parts of the Old Testament, you will find frequent allusions to a veritable cult of God's commandments, of his precepts and stipulations, which are to be pondered over day and night and thus assimilated. In the Psalms there are innumerable passages of the sort, particularly in the long Psalm 119. The Word of God, pondered over day and night, strengthens the psalmist's spirit and transforms his habits, desires and instinctive impulses: he is fashioned anew, as though re-created by assimilating the Divine Law.

This meditation on the Word of God is all the more important since we have to do it despite conditions totally alien to it, if not actually hostile: the influence of other people, of their outlook on life, of the ideologies to which they subscribe, or merely the difficulties of unfavourable situations, or of temptations which we have to overcome. God's Word has to come down into our consciences and arouse and fortify them.

On conscience, it is useful to remember that people often have very inaccurate notions about this. Often enough, people, even Christians, make a distinction between what their own conscience tells them is right and what the Church or even the Law of God tells them. People say that they cannot obey this or that ruling of the Church or of Christian morality, because it is against their conscience and because conscience should be obeyed at all times before all. Which is true, if that conscience is right and clear and if we are not merely making an excuse for behaving as we ourselves prefer. People forget that a man's conscience is usually the product of his environment and not in itself the supreme arbiter of his actions, be conditions what they may. It is easy to take refuge behind one's conscience, without considering what exactly conscience is! Conscience is the ability to judge what is good and what evil by certain conscious or unconscious criteria. We are answerable for our conscience. As Christians, we have a duty to train our conscience to conform to Christ's teachings and commands as shown in the Gospel. Conscience is precisely the result of our having assimilated the Word of God. Our conscience is never finally or completely formed; it must continually strive to reflect the Divine Law more clearly. It is, as it were, the Divine Law engraved on our heart, hence ever present to our mind, the latter being the seat of the decisions which we have to make, and these in turn engendering the habit of acting as the Gospel says we should. For us, conscience should be a light and a source of strength to help us follow the Divine Law. For it is not enough to know what is right; we have to have the strength to do it.

We now come to the third thing to be done: the need to fortify our freedom, so that we are able to act in the way that conscience indicates that we should. Such is Christian obedience to the Word of God, which must gradually transform our normal behaviour.

Finally, there is a much more personal, practical and immediate kind of obedience, that is to say, obedience to a vocation. This affects a large number of people, when we think how God's designs are achieved in history through the unfolding of our individual lives. A man who realises that he has a vocation, knows that he must obey it in one way or another. One cannot carry out a vocation without obeying it, without seeing what it demands of one, even a vocation of the social or temporal sort. The difference between the latter sort of vocation and one to a ministry in the Church or to religious consecration lies in the fact that these last involve, in one way or another, making ourselves entirely and more directly available to Christ, our professional activities included. At this degree of obedience, the mutually intimate relationship with Jesus that this kind of vocation implies also implies a summons from Christ. So here we are faced with a quite special and much deeper kind of obedience, the claims of which are hard, if not impossible, to grasp except at that level where the summons occurs, that is to say, at the level of faith as lived in the human heart by the light of the Holy Spirit and under the impulsion of a love that wishes to be absolute.

Each call to a consecrated life in the Church – and hence a call to the Fraternity – implies the existence and development of a very personal relationship with Christ, for at the level of obedience to Christ's mission is where the activities appropriate to that call occur. Now Christ is not dead, Christ is alive, Christ is at work: so, that call cannot exist except within a personal relationship of friendship and conversation with Christ – a relationship exercising our faith, in the way we grasp the mystery of Christ and in the way we put our activity at his disposal. If Christ's summons were not to be seen in this light, the call to a ministry in the Church or to a consecrated life would be no different in nature from any other vocation or profession to be exercised in the service of our fellow-men. This would alter everything and would subtly impugn the importance for mankind of the Incarnation. This sort of concept seems, however, to coincide with notions current today about religious life. The result is what you might call a shifting of the centre of gravity in the religious vocation: no longer seen as proceeding from an encounter in faith with the living person of Christ, whether that be in the intimate life of the person called, or in the activities of the Church, or in those contingent on the aims of our Congregation.

And this leads us to ask how in effect the religious ideal should be exemplified in our individual lives. On the one hand, as we have said, this entails an encounter with Jesus in obedience to his summons and in response to his invitation, '*If you wish . . . come, follow me!*'[61] and on the other, the best possible performance of the apostolic mission as appropriate to each fraternity: which mission involves particular decisions varying according to the practical conditions in which this mission has to be performed. This dual translation into action of your gift of yourself to Christ, thus conditioned by time and place, will have to be different, you might say individualised, in each case and for each of you: which means that you must be continually seeking to know the practical content of God's will.

You will have hence to keep asking yourselves what God expects of you. At the same time, you will have the feeling that you have no great say in the matter, except that you are ready to obey God's will provided that you know what it is. Now, this is where the difficulty lies: how can we know what God's will is for us? Isn't everything foreordained by the will of God who called me into existence? How would Christ answer this question? Wouldn't he simply say once more, 'If you wish . . . do this, obey my law'? We do not have to renounce either our intellect or our free-will in the quest to discover what God's plan is for us. Man was not created free, intelligent, bearing the image of God within him, to be fated at a given moment, even when confronted with a divine message, to abdicate both intellect and freedom of choice by passively executing a design imposed on him. I do not see how we can justify this sort of passive concept of obedience to God.

The quest for the content of God's will is therefore a work incumbent on the conscience of every individual, in the perspective of a recognised vocation and with the assistance of the Holy Spirit. This help is with us while we search and strengthens us to do so, but is no miraculous substitute for the search itself. We are given the light of faith to guide us, and openhearted love to practise what we discover. But, you will object, this sort of search is only possible when concerned with the application of some universal law. As concerns my personal vocation, how could I possibly know what the content of God's will may be? Indeed, on joining the Fraternity, after some experience, having given thought and taken advice, you may conclude, 'Yes, the Lord has called me here.' But would the Lord have actually told you so? Would you have received a clear revelation from heaven? Or would a Superior or spiritual director have told you, 'In God's name I can assure you that you have a vocation'? He would be a very rash man who did tell you that and might very easily be mistaken.

No, you have to try and look at this clearly, as you would any other sort of decision, taking all that attracts you, your desires and your talents, into account.

Among the supernatural factors, there are also the interior promptings of the Holy Spirit, urging you. Discreet as a whisper,[62] which is very easily stifled, or violent as a storm-wind,[63] bearing all before it, the Spirit of Jesus prompts us on, while leaving us with complete freedom to recognise its genuineness and to respond to it. Christ's summons, however, because of what it contains, is bound to turn our lives upside down. The quest for God's design can never cease, since the design will go on unfolding its secrets right to the end of our lives. The fraternities may make mistakes and stupid decisions, may despite their good intentions commit themselves in doubtful directions which they will have to reconsider; and our own behaviour as Little Brothers or religious will be far from perfect. And this is why we shall have to keep on reconsidering our conduct in the light of constant meditation on the Word and by trying our best to understand God's design for the Fraternity and for each one of us as individuals.

Do not suppose that each of us has a sort of predetermined role which will gradually be revealed to us, we only having to accept it. The plan of our lives should be the fruit of search in the Holy Spirit. Man is capable of this, he has a duty to do this, since God has made him responsible for his own actions and hence for his decisions and plans. We are still responsible for ourselves, even in fulfilling a vocation intimately linked to Christ, in its origin as in its unfolding. For it is a fact, as we have already said, that every vocation to the consecrated religious life, like every vocation to a mission in the Church, puts us into direct and personal relationship with the living Christ, he being free to reveal himself in his Church, in the progress and manifestations of the Kingdom of God in the world at large, as in the depths of the individual heart. This personalisation of Providence in the unfolding of our vocation does not stop each of us, while putting ourselves at the service of God's plan, from having to seek out what that plan requires by using our brains and wills, both God-given. The way we conduct the search presupposes that we really understand our vocation: for that must provide the light by which we proceed. Our vocation is offered us by the Church and the Fraternity, that vocation being the fruit of a charism conferred by the Holy Spirit on the Church and authenticated by the latter. Although received from the Church and the Fraternity, our vocation is never imposed on us as a sort of ready-made plan to be accepted by us without asking questions.

In discharging our religious vocation, we are helped by the Spirit of Jesus. Christian destiny, the design revealed to us by God in his Son, the design of adoption and salvation, is carried out in unpredictable, undetermined ways in each human life. Here we see the mysterious meeting-point between God's freedom and human freedom. Even the task of evangelism is not determined in advance, as far as its practical manifestations are concerned. This is left to our freedom of action. You have only to see how people use this freedom, how they can waste it and how admirably they can succeed in its use – even though we are by no means shielded from misjudgment or the risks attendant on any human enterprise.

And so it is too with our holiness – a word which seems to be falling out of use, though I cannot think of another word to replace it! If we are faithful in meditating on the Word of God and assiduous in prayer, we shall be in as permanent a state of union with Christ as we can be, and he will sensitise us to the promptings of the Holy Spirit. We shall then be able to receive the light of the Spirit, to acquire the wisdom of the children of God, which consists in being able to see things in God's light and to judge our actions by the teachings of the Gospel. And thus we can acquire that Gospel prudence, which is a mental habit of judging all things, especially our actions, by the light of the Holy Spirit. For I must insist on this, it is we who do the judging – with our brains. If you are short on commonsense, if you leap before you look, if your judgment is influenced, and thus clouded, by emotion, if you cannot humbly trust other people's judgment, you will extinguish the Spirit within you. Some people will tend to act in too much of hurry; others will adopt too logical an approach; others again will show undue passivity in accepting the mentality of the environment. Trusting in the Holy Spirit does not dispense you from following your own judgment; you are always and altogether responsible for your own life. Living it properly depends on you. And so does your proper performance of the evangelist's task.

Christian wisdom, the ability to judge like Christ, will grow in you thanks to the light of faith, which light the heart discovers in God's silence and in renunciation of the world. Let your view of men and things not be clouded or arrested by the immediate foreground view of those tangible things and events ever pressing for attention. When taking photographs, you set the focus either for infinity or for close-up. Things can hardly be in focus at both long range and in close-up, unless the light is very strong indeed. So it is with us: instinctively we focus on the foreground. Most people habitually focus on the foreground, that is, on the immediate present and on the things that need doing here and now. For them, the perspectives of the infinite are so blurred as to be lost to view.

The contemplative who, contrariwise, fixes his view on the infinite, risks losing his footing in the immediate present with its concrete demands; he has a kind of myopia over temporal things. You need an extra amount of contemplative light to come by sufficient wisdom and prudence to allow you to focus simultaneously on the infinite and the foreground. Wisdom and prudence consist precisely in projecting the infinite view on to present, practical problems. They illuminate the decisions we have to take, which in turn allow us, in the freedom of heart which renunciation of the world assures, to remain involved in human affairs while we are also attuned to the intentions of the Author of the Kingdom of God. We have to attain to sharing Jesus's attitudes to the redemption and salvation of mankind. Thus we can become poor and humble servants of Christ's design. A clear view of that design and how it must be carried out will inform our minds, our free decisions and our personal and communal activities in the Fraternity. And this will be true for any religious in his Congregation too.

The wisdom guiding our intellectual gaze and the prudence shaping our decisions are both likely to play us false if they are not confronted by the wisdom and prudence of others, if our focus is not corrected by that other people. This is why, in the Fraternity as in all religious life, the concept and way of leading the common life as a Christian community requires the pooling of spiritual goods. The pooling of material goods is secondary to the sharing and mutual communication of spiritual goods. Without the unity which comes from sharing the life at its inward level the pooling of material goods is powerless to create a genuine Christian community. Mutual communication at the level of life according to the Spirit postulates detachment from our own ideas, humility of heart and mind, attention to others and willingness to listen to other people's judgment, in the conviction that we can really enlighten one another. This is what a Christian community is all about – otherwise it would be idle to talk about co-responsibility.

What exactly do we mean today when we talk about co-responsibility in the religious life? Is it compatible with the religious obedience which, we believe, sums up our consecration to God? Let us say for a start that the tendency to emphasise an attitude of co-responsibility can be regarded as a step in the right direction, in so far as it comes from a new awareness of what a Christian community requires. And indeed this is consistent with human fact and Christ's design: that each should be responsible for his brothers – yes, in more senses than one. I am not only talking about that vast sharing of life taking place in the communion of saints, for of this we are often unaware and it hardly affects our concept of human life. This communion takes place at the level of intercession and of a sense of responsibility for the salvation of all men, each of us playing our part in atoning for evil. Our participation in Christ's death will consist in our sacrificing our lives, by means of the crosses on our way, and in so making our lives one endless intercession, because we truly feel that we are part and parcel of the whole human race. We must discover this sense of solidarity binding us to each and all of our fellow-men, all dedicated to building the same ideal city on earth, but even more must we discover that other solidarity binding us to them in Christ, with Christ, to complete Christ's mission. This discovery we have to keep on making, and it will colour the way we behave towards others and, more deeply, our human relationships within the Christian community.

You have already experienced what I am going to say, and you will experience it again and again: it is not easy to attune our human relationships to the demands of the human and the Christian community, since the relationships are subject to the stresses of instinctive likes and dislikes, of uncontrollable exasperation, of that thick – you might say heavy – wall of partition always tending to isolate us from one another. Out of weariness, we take the line of least resistance and so run the risk of forgetting that a continual effort on our part to meet our fellow-men is one of Christ's abiding demands. Since this meeting is a work of patience, of constantly starting again, it is never finished. If we idealise it to the point of no longer behaving in a sensible way, no longer accepting reality for what it is, we shall, by making impossible demands, almost certainly become discouraged, and we shall in the meanwhile have made other people lose heart too. The creation of a truly Christian community is a never completely realised ideal, which we have to keep on striving to attain and in which every member of the Fraternity has his or her part to play in the building up of a brotherly community.

Contrariwise, if by co-responsibility we mean the fact that no one member of the religious community is ultimately responsible for its well-being and that it has no other source of authority than the unanimous or majority opinion of its members, this idea is based on a misconception leaving the specific nature of religious consecration out of account as the constituent link in religious life which creates the ecclesial community. You must understand this: the observance of religious obedience is something unique in itself, its motivation lying in our most personal relationships with God. But this obedience is wedded, so to speak, to a human fact, i.e. that there can be no society without authority. This is obvious. People who deny the need for authority, whether in the Church or in a religious Congregation, do so in the name of an unrealistic and utopian concept of Christian society – a concept very different from that of Christ, who did not make the same mistake. The apostles first gathered round Jesus because of his appeal. Each was thus bound to him by this very strong, personal appeal; Jesus gradually organised this group; he appointed one of them to be its leader. Similarly, as local Churches later came into being, they too always had their leaders. The Apostle Paul shows us in his letters that the organising of these communities was often marked by disputes and rivalries; in such cases, the problems were referred to Paul's authority. It would be taking a somewhat supernaturalistic view, in the pejorative sense of the word, to imagine that a Christian community, still less a more restricted religious community, should not be subject to the normal laws governing natural and civil societies. A religious community cannot be geared to the highest claims of contemplative love and apostolic activity unless it is a properly balanced human society in the first place. The spiritual and religious life has already suffered too much from a supernaturalistic concept of perfection, resulting in neglect of values which are natural and basic to all types of social existence. True, these natural claims are never easy to meet and are seldom satisfied. We are perfectly aware that none of us are as we should wish ourselves to be, and we never find other people to be as we should like them to be either. The ideal notion of the Christian community, when based on what human relationships ought to be if Christian charity were one hundred per cent effective, is bound to be imperfect and to fall short of what hope reveals that the future city will be like. For the qualities of that city can only be occasionally and fleetingly captured on earth. And so it is with the smaller family-type unit, the indissoluble links within which ought normally to express that ideal of loving unity held up by Christ to his disciples.

There are certain privileged moments – when, for instance, we are in retreat before God – when brotherly communion and the joy of being together become almost tangible. We could wish our life were always like this. But then reality comes blundering in with its daily pressures of sluggishness, obstacles and opposition. We all know this. The dream of a community without a head, without a leader, comes largely from an idealised view of reality. But if we start from reality as it actually is, I do not see what more could be achieved or how a Christian or religious community could be more perfect or more truly itself if it did not have a leader or head. One of the reasons for obeying, even in a religious society, is to share in the common good, and to do this we consent to bow to its claims. Any properly balanced society requires the acceptance of a minimum of discipline and order, and hence of obedience, provided that the collective effort is properly directed to the common aim of that community and is not arbitrarily exerted.

And here, a question occurs to me. In the religious life, obedience to a Superior is not the main thing but is a part of obedience to a vocation, to the service of which that authority is pledged too. And this is why, over the centuries, the modes of exercising this authority, the better to serve the purpose, have given rise to varied forms of government in the Church and particularly in religious Orders. The service of authority, you see, was adapted to the differing needs and attitudes of the times. History shows a range of styles of government, from those of the patriarchal or monarchical type to those most democratic or most centralised, depending on the way of life and activities, whether apostolic, charitable or contemplative, of the communities concerned. These forms of government frequently reflected the political patterns of the day. Which underlines the fact that religious society obeys exactly the same laws ordinarily governing people when they are trying to organise any society, by developing the individual sense of responsibility in all its members with a view to producing a better form of government. This need to keep the form of government constantly under review so as to make it more appropriate to its purpose has always characterised the Church, even at its most exalted levels.

Changes in the way institutions are organised become necessary from time to time and this entails a right and duty to self-criticism as a permanent but not necessarily painful or harmful feature of institutional life. You have to have it. Christians and pastors of the Church alike are always human, and the Church as a society is always subject to those stresses inherent in any other human society. But it is none the less true for all that, that hidden within the life, activities and government of the Church and inextricably mixed up with all its human characteristics, reside the life, activities and authority of Christ. This is a mystery, that is, a reality only accessible to the eye of faith. In the Church and her methods of government there will always be something totally other than what is immediately apparent about her way of exercising authority. Naturally, it is very easy to lose our awareness of this fact, given the pressure of the human factor, as also the sometimes insurmountable difficulty we find in focusing our gaze, not on the human foreground, but on the divine infinity intermingled with it. We have already said this, so I shall not go into it again, especially since the strictures which can be levelled against the way religious authority is exercised are numberless – and so we should be wasting our time, since you know what those strictures are as well as I do. You have only to listen to what other people say, or to read what is constantly being written in the papers – things which have been repeated year after year. The same goes for the religious life, which we are talking about now. There are plenty of reasons for complaint, there is no denying that: abuse of authority, a tendency to paternalism or to maternalism as the case may be, the state of arrested adolescence in which religious are kept since they have not had the benefit of a community environment conducive to the full development of their personalities. Yes, and plenty of other complaints too!

But could things really be otherwise, given that we are talking about men and women? God alone can answer that! All these abuses of authority cannot prevent the human basis of authority and the social organisation of religious communities in the Church from having a quite special nature, on account of the fact that this organisation and government are the manifestation and presence of Christ's own authority. Thus we have to make a constant effort of renewal, so that religious society does not betray the truth to which by its existence it bears witness.

So now you see why the Prior and his officers in the Fraternity are not mere organs co-ordinating what the membership at large may think, nor yet a secretariat synthesising the results of general discussion. There may be a tendency to see the functions of officials in this guise. But the thing to hang on to as a positive guide is our progress towards the concept of an authority which is prepared to listen before taking decisions. This more democratic style of government does not mean that it is not basically germane to the Church or that it does not derive its authority from Christ. By the same token however, it must not be allowed to degenerate into government by the assent of the majority. Preliminary consideration of what will serve the greatest good, preparatory reflection on what decisions ought to be taken, must be planned in such a way that all concerned can take part in them; the decisions thus taken will be the best possible in the circumstances and everyone will be personally committed to making them work. This preliminary research, however, must also be conducted by the light of faith and in awareness of the community's religious identity – as should be the case in the Church at large. The arbitrary decisions of a superior who does not consult his religious and is out of touch with them and who makes decisions before appreciating the situation and the nature of the problems involved, can cause a great deal of trouble and certainly harm the members of the community. We have already emphasised that the content of the Divine Will cannot be found without our using our heads, and then is only mediated through our brains. The role of officers of the Church does not exempt them from obeying the laws of nature, nor from doing everything within their power to become wise and make intelligent preparation before deciding what will be best. Were they not to do so, the responsibility when things subsequently go wrong would lie with them, since they might have avoided this by adopting a different view of how to wield their authority.

Experience over the last few years has clearly shown us that renewal along these lines is an excellent thing. The rediscovery of these obligations may have made a religious superior's job rather harder. On the other hand, the sincere acceptance of his authority is more secure, since it builds up a true community spirit. All religious authority in the Church of Christ, wielded in the spirit of Christ, should be aimed at uniting the members of the Church, that is to say, in our case, the members of the Fraternity. In a community animated by brotherly love, mutual respect, care for the good of the next man and a sense of apostolic purpose, lucidity of judgment strengthened by the light of faith and by the gifts of the Holy Spirit is normally shared by everyone. St Benedict said that an abbot should summon the community whenever there was important business to transact. '*The reason why we ask for all the brothers to be summoned to deliberate is this: that God often inspires the youngest with the best suggestions.*[64] As you see, there is nothing new under the sun; but it must be admitted that for some time past people have overlooked the importance of listening to what other people had to say, as they have also overlooked the fact that all are summoned to collaborate in finding out how to put God's designs into effect for and by means of their community.

We must also recognise that there used, especially in the last century, to be a notion that a superior's charisma tended to authenticate the content of the orders he gave, whatever that content might be, on the sole grounds that those orders emanated from authority. From the moment a superior decided on something, that became God's will as far as the religious was concerned. So it did not really matter what the content was, since the moment the superior spoke, what he said was expressing the will of God. Now, this notion is a false one and based on confused thinking. What is certain is that, if I wish to fulfil the law of obedience as I have vowed to do, I am obliged to obey my superior even if, as St Paul says, he is mediocre. But this does not imply that what the superior has decided is automatically the best possible decision and hence consistent with God's designs. God's will, however, is that I obey. People used to forget from time to time how serious the superior's obligation was to reach the best decision. And this is what is guaranteed, humanly speaking, by the practice of prior consultation in an atmosphere of co-responsibility.

As an ideal, this is clear and straightforward! But in practice, things are very different! It is a hard and arduous task to arrive in the harmony of faith at a relationship between authority and obedience which truly expresses the mystery of Christ. The concept of obedience in religious life is something specifically Christian and only conceivable in terms of faith in Christ. This is not true of human societies. In a religious Congregation, the superior derives his authority from the Church.

So the question then arises as to what the nature of this authority is. This is not without importance, for there are several types of authority in the Church, and correspondingly different types of obedience. First and foremost, there is that authority vested in the Church as guardian of the faith. This authority touches the difficult and delicate domain of intellectual obedience, which is accorded in faith when the Church affirms a truth guaranteed by God and to which the human intellect must conform. Then, there is the authority of the Church's pastors as guides of the Christian conscience and leaders of the Churches which they have been called to found and govern. This also commands the obedience of the faithful, though the claims and limits of this obedience are more difficult to define. But religious life is charismatic, in the sense of being generated spontaneously by an impulse of the Holy Spirit, and as such does not depend on the hierarchy, though the latter has to test its genuineness. The authority of the superior of a Congregation and that of those other officers deriving authority from him is thus of a different kind from that belonging to the hierarchical Church and is neither an emanation of nor a delegation from the latter. Although authenticated and confirmed by the hierarchy, the authority of a religious superior is still a charismatic one, since this authority is entrusted to him for the purpose of fulfilling the aim and mission of a community brought into existence within the Church by charismatic means. Once this society has been authenticated by the Church, that is, has been accepted by her as serving her over-all mission, the Church entrusts this charismatic kind of life to the authority of a superior. Religious obedience, in so far as it is accepted by the religious as identifying him with Christ's obedience to his Father, is charismatic too. Hence, the choice of a superior lies with each religious Congregation according to its constitutions, and not with the hierarchy of the Church. The Church however con-

firms the choice of superior, as also his authority, since as soon
as there is a community of the faithful the Church legitimately
assumes pastoral responsibility for that community. The
religious life offers a kind of meeting-point between an
organised charismatic movement and service to the Church.
The Church exercises her pastorate over religious communities as over all other Christians. The Church is responsible for the lives of her faithful, and for the Church a group of
faithful is what we are.

Every religious society is authenticated by the Church, not
only however as a road to evangelical perfection, but also as an
apostolic organisation with more or less specialised aims. And
under this dual aspect, the Council defined the consecrated
religious life as a gift from the Holy Spirit to the Church.[65]   I
do not think that we by our own unaided critical endeavours
can re-invent a state and style of life orginally the work of the
Holy Spirit. We cannot close our ears to this teaching. Read
the Conciliar documents over again. I for my part cannot imagine religious life in its fundamental aspects in any other way
than the Church presents it to me: which does not of course
exclude the need for a constant effort of renewal and for
creativity at the practical level. But we do not need to invent
what is presented to us in the Church and interpreted by the
Church, witnessing to long tradition and invested with the
charismatic responsibility of guiding us along these paths.
What the Church tells us about religious life in the documents
of the last Council deserves study and reflection: '*The state of
life constituted by profession of the evangelical counsels, though not a
part of the hierarchical structure of the Church, is inseparably a part of
the Church's life and holiness.*'[66]

After these initial considerations I now come to the practical
consequences as they affect you individually. And this is what
matters for you. What do you think about obedience? What
do you feel about it in your heart? Intentions and ineffectual
resolutions are not enough. As the Apostle James wrote, '*To
listen to the word and not obey is like looking at your own features in a
mirror and then, after a quick look, going off and immediately forgetting
what you look like.*'[67] Here in the peace of Brother Charles's
hermitage, you can contemplate your vocation by the light of
adoration of the mystery of Jesus in the Blessed Sacrament,

during these happy days when nothing comes to hinder your good desires. But when you go back to your fraternities, what will it be like then? Will you forget the discoveries you have made and contemplated in the light of Divine Truth?

It is the same thing with obedience as with prayer or any other Christian characteristic: it has to be built up as a reality within us by a constant effort of renewal. We have to be prepared to keep on starting again, not only because we get in a rut and stop reacting – which is negative – but also because we keep changing. Such is life: situations change, but we too change very radically. Your way of obeying will inevitably change as you grow older. In the old days, young religious were generally considered to be more obedient than old ones. Although no one would ever be tempted to say such a thing today, it is certainly desirable that an old religious should obey better than a novice! He will often obey in a different way. With experience and the maturing of our lives in relation to God and our brothers, we cannot help obeying differently. When obedience means the active participation of our will in the mystery of Christ's obedience, it touches us very deeply and affects our ability to employ our lives as we think fit. Our view of things changes with passing time. Obedience taken seriously inevitably has repercussions on our inner, personal lives and on our relationship with Jesus. For there is a hidden love at this degree of intimacy, which God alone can measure. Do I truly want to enter the mystery of Christ's obedience so deeply as to associate myself with it in every one of my activites? Is my love for Christ sufficiently strong and clear-sighted for me to wish to submit to this obedience? This may perhaps extravagant and unrelated to any obvious result. Yes, we are talking of the folly of obedience to death, to death on the Cross. We mean dying to ourselves, to our desires. Must we not try all the time to deepen our obedience, in step with our fervour and our growing love? For a religious truly to fulfil his vocation, obedience must be as deep as that. It presupposes an apprenticeship of faith, a renewal of our deepest intentions, a reappraisal of habits already acquired and experience of the Cross.

In the Fraternity, the growth of the common good of a fraternity, as of the Fraternity taken as a whole – a growth which authority has the job of translating into fact, of making possible by embodying it in human relationships – must be the matter of that obedience which we pledge to Jesus. This obedience would remain as something merely desired or planned, had it no possibility of being expressed by our actions. What should we have done, had we been called to follow Jesus along the roads of Galilee? Should we have put our lives, our possessions and our time at his disposal? Jesus said very clearly to those who offered him their services, *'Put your nets aside, leave your father's house, sell your possessions, renounce your very self, then come with me.'* Jesus would have sent us where he wanted, he would have told us what to say and do to serve his mission. Isn't that what we should have wanted? We cannot want anything less, twenty centuries later. And in and through the Church we can make this same gift of our lives to Jesus, to serve his mission. Now there are intermediaries, but they too are part of Christ's plan and they are charged with this mission as it affects us. In religious life, our superiors are invested with the mission of making that charism effective, which in turn contains the charism of obedience to Christ, an obedience which is meant to be like this and to which those offering themselves to the Fraternity have been called. To them, the Church puts the same question as Christ would: 'If you wish it, this is the way.'

Where then do we stand? Let us face up to reality. What do we see? God alone knows the heart and its intentions; all we can do is observe the actual effects of obedience in our community relationships. Sometimes the people in charge allow the brothers to do as they please, and avoid giving orders of any sort. Respecting the freedom of each member, they confine themselves to co-ordinating their efforts. There is also the passivity of well-disposed brothers, who do not refuse obedience but wait for the man in charge to take the initiative. If nothing is asked of them, they go on as before, not refusing anything but without feeling the need to encounter any expression of God's will. Their desire to obey in a general way is sincere. Perhaps the majority are like this? And besides relations with superiors, there are the claims made by the brotherly life, of a sharing that obliges us to take account of other people, to accept their point of view, their needs. And there are brothers who actively take the initiative in seeking out obedience, since they have discovered the need for it through contemplating the heart of Christ and the mystery of his presence in the Church. Obedience cannot in fact be conceived of except as active, as a continual effort to achieve union with the one we love. True religious obedience cannot be passive. Obeying on a specific instance consists in taking ourselves in hand to give ourselves, and this entails our being aware of our vocation to identify ourselves with Christ, who was obedient even to dying on the Cross: and aware that this way of obeying disposes us to be saviours with Jesus.

In the absence of the requisite conditions, whether as regards the general attitude of mind of the brothers or as regards the attitude of the superiors, for conscious and responsible obedience to be possible, obedience will stay no more than an intention hidden in the heart, since it will not find the means of translating itself into action, sufficient response being lacking among our brothers. Superiors may be disinclined to exert their authority, may think it preferable to let things go on as they are, or to encourage discussion among the brothers without giving any final decision for which they can be held clearly responsible. In circumstances like these, people athirst to give themselves in religious obedience will probably get discouraged. Desire for obedience motivated by love can easily fade for lack of opportunity to express itself. Obviously, it is essential that this sort of obedience should be freely desired and willed. It is possible that this desire will not exist to begin with; it is something which has to be discovered by the light of faith in the mystery of Christ alive and active in the Church. But the ideal should be held up as an essential element of our consecrated life.

This type of obedience must not be confused with merely practising a discipline, keeping a rule or even with submitting to the obligations of the common life. In the latter, there would be submission, respect for other people, but not free obedience. Confusion between these two attitudes, too often both designated discipline, causes many problems. For the majority of those who embrace the religious life have from their earliest years suffered from being crushed, pushed about and subjected to all sorts of discipline, the many constraints of life; regimentation at work, traffic control and all sorts of other assaults on our freedom and spontaneity have begotten a re-

jectionist attitude, if not reactions of revolt to any form of constraint imposed from outside.

There is thus a transition to be effected, a training to be un-
dergone, to discover what demands true liberty makes. And
this cannot be had without the freely willed constraints of a
liberating obedience. Many people find this a difficult path today. Obedience has been subjected to so many distortions,
weakening and enslaving our will – not setting it free. And this
is why I say that an attitude of genuine obedience, expressive
of a great love, is not granted to begin with. Nor must we call
obedience that ability shown by a few to let other people
manage them: these are good-natured people, thought
suitable to lead the common life because they do what they are
told without getting upset. This ability may of course be the
foundation of a genuine loving availability, but this is not invariably so. Others, on the other hand, will experience great
problems over obedience and the common life; they find it
hard to give up their personal opinions. The young often
evince a need for a common life, for a very tight group-ex-
istence, but this does not always entail a search for true
obedience. In some cases rather the reverse. This need for a
common life often conceals a lack of maturity or inability to
handle life in adult terms. Hence the instinctive, vital need to
be carried along by other people. Now, no one who cannot
manage his own life is capable of obeying either. Obedience is
a gift freely given, which means that you must be in full
possession of yourself.

The progress of each individual is therefore very important
and it can only be freely willed. Obedience not freely desired
and sought or received as loving and willing communion with
Christ, cannot be imposed. That is impossible! The state of
mind of the modern generation will make that progress slow
and tentative. And on the other hand, the day to day community requirements of religious life presuppose an initial
minimum acceptance of a common project and of freely
accepted discipline. This is one of the fundamental difficulties
encountered in modern religious life, leading some people to
question the foundations of religious life as such.

In the life of a consecrated religious, the obedience which is
loving freedom gives us the assurance of being able to dare
what we should not dare to do, were it not for obedience. To

lay down our life in obedience to Christ means being assured that so absolute a giving of ourselves is possible for us to make. Faith tells us that, God being what he is, giving ourselves to him means that absolute, life-long gift embodied in the religious life. Now, perhaps we feel incapable of making such a gift, and therefore are not capable of making it. If this gift had to depend on our own decision, we might well hesitate. When I am constantly thrown back on my own initiative for every decision, for choosing my commitment, for choosing what mission to pursue, what fraternity to join, I am reduced to my own resources. What absolute am I likely to encounter if I have to make all my decisions on my own? Yet, if I receive my mission out of obedience, if this is confirmed or commissioned by the Church then I can put a love and strength far surpassing my own into my response since, even if I may in fact make mistakes, a light, a decision has intervened which makes me say: I am responding to Christ's will by accepting this kind of life, this mission, which I should not have dared to choose on my own. The knowledge that I am doing my own will is not what is going to strengthen me. Of course, if you ask me, I shall say what I personally should like, and where my aspirations and talents lie, and this is perfectly in order; there is co-operation in the search. But beyond this, I shall go, not towards what I have chosen because I have chosen it, but because I have been sent by my Superior in the Church's name. I should not dare to commit myself if I had not been sent. It is a far finer thing to make my life a practical gift to Christ, unhesitating, daring all for him and with him; for, if I run into difficulties, I shall then be entitled to shout to the Lord that these are his concern, since I dared to confront them for his sake. Thus it was with the prophets. In a life consecrated to evangelism, this is of capital importance and I am afraid that sometimes people lose sight of it.

It must be admitted: on principles we can all be agreed and I do not think, even at the present time, that many people really question the fundamentals of religious life or the fact that obedience is one essential element of it. But where the differences begin is when it comes to putting principles into practice; then people forget that the call to the religious life requires us to make a break with our former life, whereas people too often tend to want to incorporate all the qualities of the worldly into the consecrated life. A climate of freedom is not only not opposed to obedience but actually favours it since, once again, obedience cannot be imposed: or it is no longer obedience being required but the discipline of common life or action.

I am not saying there is no need for a minimum of discipline. But this is needed for other reasons than obedience. If I assert that it is useful or necessary for the sake of harmonious brotherly life and perseverance in prayer to observe some sort of order in the common life, to have set times for doing certain things, should I invoke obedience to Christ or more sensibly emphasise that these procedures are imposed out of respect for my brothers and because a minimum of discipline is essential to a peaceful common life? It is true that in one school of spirituality, these observances would have been imposed as an act of obedience to Christ. Was it better that way? It may be that a brother will feel impelled to make these humble daily efforts in the spirit of obedience to God. But I should not prompt my brothers to do so unless I felt that they were ready to practise their faithfulness in little things at this altruistic level. Some rules and observances are needed to ensure discipline in the common life, and too frequent a staking of the consecration of my will to Christ in trivial matters like these can easily lead to a fading of my vocational ideals. It is unrealistic to put actions of varying importance all on the same footing and to confuse the reasons for doing them by ascribing all to obedience. Which does not alter the fact that obedience is the way in which our lives are consecrated to Christ. And this fundamental and constant attitude of obedience is what contemplation of Christ should establish and maintain in our hearts.

IX

Consecrated to God and his Christ in the Church

A fitting way of concluding these reflections on your religious vocation is to remind you in a word or two about the nature of your promises to the Church and of the consecration which is their effect. The possibility which the Church now offers Religious Institutes of replacing first, temporary vows by a simple promise or some other form of undertaking indicates that thought has been given to the nature of the change which will ensue. What are the reasons behind this? What are the effects of this act on your relationship with God? We are not dealing now with a mere choice of words, nor are we engaging in theoretical discussion over the distinctions between promises, vows and undertakings. When we express an intention, and above all when the Church does so, relying on the experience of men of God, we should believe that this has bearing on something real enough to affect our lives. The Church has recognised our Fraternity as a religious congregation. We have always wanted to be religious, consecrated by perpetual profession in the sense that the Church understands this. On the eve of pronouncing our vows, I think we should do well briefly to recapitulate what these imply and what they involve.

First, I may say that they may be regarded as fulfilling that consecration which we received by baptism. They represent a new commitment to the Lord, with special and specific content, since they bear on the concrete realities of our lives. This commitment only makes sense for someone who has been baptised but is relevant at a different level from baptism: the perfection of charity. Baptism puts us in a state to realise this, but does not in itself achieve it.

The ability to become sons of God and to behave as sons of God is conferred by baptism. But we still have to live up to the requirements of this state. Filial behaviour is conferred, though only as a seed. Baptism, conferred once, is the beginning of an existence characterised by growth, continual evolution, vital energy. The seed of divine sonship placed in the newly baptised Christian as a leaven of filial life and universal love is in a state of suspended development. We have to develop these potentialities and translate them into actions: and this is entirely our own responsibility, weak and sinful though we be. And then we receive God's summons, and we respond by pledging ourselves to the religious state. Let this be clear: it is wrong and contrary to the whole experience of the Church to represent baptism and religious consecration as inconsistent with each other.

If I want to grasp the true significance of religious vows, it is no use my considering them at this or that stage of their being put into practice, nor my limiting myself to canonical or theological definitions of them; I have to accept them as they have actually been practised everywhere, throughout the history of religious life in the Church. And first, I shall see that they have an absolute and final character, since they are addressed to God who is himself eternal and absolute. I do not think that profession in the religious state was originally conceived of as being temporary. The idea of temporary vows is comparatively late. These were introduced because a probationary period was found necessary and because of decisions taken by the Council of Trent to cover all the new Institutes springing up but no longer conforming to the type of monastic life hitherto governed by the great monastic Rules recognised by the Church.

The only true and ultimate motive for profession is to respond to the claims of love. Now, all love worthy of the name wants to be absolute. It is in the nature of God, when he calls us, to expect a response on our part unqualified by either time or place – if you will pardon the expression – as far as our lives are concerned. Our whole existence, every dimension of our lives forever, is what we offer to our God. To Him from whom we have received all, to Him who is Love itself, to Him who is the eternal Source of our lives, we cannot make a limited, temporal response; this would not make sense. This is what gives our commitment its strength and makes it what it ought to be. When we talk about a covenant between God and man, this is by definition final.

Take the Old Covenant for example. We might accurately say that it was concerned with the fulfilling of promises bounded by historic time and geographical space: the establishing of a people, their liberation from captivity and their installation in a given territory. The promise was indeed limited in time, if it is interpreted in terms of a temporal kingdom. And we know that this interpretation of messianism was precisely the one which Christ refuted: the Divine Covenant was of universal and eternal scope. The transition from the carnal Israel preoccupied with hopes of an earthly kingdom, to the spiritual Israel, to the Church of Christ, was acutely painful for the Chosen People. Many Jews still accord great significance to the Covenant. So it is with the covenant concluded in religious life between the person called and the God inviting him to expand his love to the dimensions of eternity. We must not be content with limiting the covenant of profession to a temporary commitment or a temporary task. We should be making the same mistake as those Jews who could not see their way to accepting the messianic covenant as pertaining to an ultimate and universal kingdom.

That mysterious Old Testament book, the *Song of Solomon*, is at once a love song and a song in praise of fidelity. Religious consecration is often compared to marriage on account of the absolute and final character conferred on this consecration by the infinite love of God entering into alliance with our poor, fragile, finite love.

Religious commitment takes the form of promises made to God. Now, a promise made to God is a vow. Whichever word you use, it comes to the same thing. What is characteristic of the religious profession is that it takes place in the Church, where it is publicly received and confirmed by those who have received pastoral and sacerdotal power. As the Church is a society, it is natural that this commitment to God should take a form consistent with the laws of that society and with those of the community erected by the Church into a religious Congregation. The effects of this commitment are therefore not entirely private; they are juridically defined in terms of obligations to Church and to community. But this does not stop these promises from having been made to God. Being made in union with other people, with a community, they naturally entail reciprocal agreements, which themselves naturally have to be defined.

Any Christian may find himself bound by a promise made to God in his heart. This is no one else's concern; whereas there is a public aspect to religious profession, which means that this commitment concerns the Church as a community; hence the Church accepts and authenticates it. It is not a secret commitment. The community and the Church are guarantors of your commitment, and they define the obligations incurred. Hence this is an ecclesial act. If juridical forms are necessary, these are of secondary importance. Juridical forms do not constitute profession; they deal with the consequences at community level implicit in the vows themselves.

The value of the act of religious profession can only be rightly appreciated in so far as we have faith in the Church. If my faith in the Church does not lead me to believe with all my heart in the Church's power to authenticate my mission in Christ's name, to offer it in union with Christ's priestly act of sacrifice, to bind and loose consciences in Christ's name, if – in a word – the Church is not Christ alive on earth for me, obviously I shall not see any difference between the consecration of religious profession and that resulting from a private promise, or even from a personal determination to live my life according to the Gospel without making any, even private, undertakings of any sort at all. I think we need not scruple to say that where there is a weakening of faith in the Church or a questioning of the Church's powers, there, to the same degree, we find the true value of and very reason for religious life also being impugned.

Some people may ask: What is the point of making vows? Wouldn't it be alright to join a community without making promises, and live conscientiously by the Gospel? This is undeniably a truly Christian thing to do. But it is a different vocation from ours. That does not stop the Holy Spirit from inspring a different kind of life in the Church: I mean, religious consecration. This is a fact which we should respect. Yet, because of the consequences which the Church attaches to religious profession, because of the seriousness of a promise binding forever, because this covenantal bond is so grave that only the Church has power to unbind it, it is natural that perpetual profession should be preceded by a period of preparation, taking different forms in different circumstances, as for instance simple vows in monastic life before the taking of solemn vows, or temporary vows in other religious institutes. People have latterly become more aware of the fundamental difference which exists between temporary vows and perpetual profession. The former are a preparation, temporary by definition, a progression towards perpetual profession, which for its part is final and unique.

The trend now observable in the Church to replace temporary vows by some other kind of promise originated on the one hand from a wish to attach importance to the concept of consecration by vows which in themselves had to be final, and on the other from the unwillingness often felt by the young to commit themselves at once by pronouncing vows sanctioned by the Church. There is a need, it is now felt, for a progression towards perpetual profession.

The recent Chapter defined the nature of temporary probation in the Fraternity of Little Brothers of the Gospel. First, this temporary period is only to be served once: it cannot be renewed, and either ends in perpetual profession or in withdrawal from the Fraternity. It is thus well and truly a progression towards perpetual profession. But, to be a proper preparation for this, the temporary commitment, being the initial response to God, must also be made to God. Some institutes prefer to make this probation into a commitment to the community or institute, the rules of which the probationer promises to obey. I frankly do not see how one can prepare for perpetual profession without making a promise of chastity, nor do I see how this could be made to anyone other than God. I do this in response to God' summons. The primary aim of a religious Congregation, after all, is the consecration of its members to God. If I begin my journey in the Fraternity, I do this in response to a call from God, to consecrate my life to him.

But, you may say, if this first commitment involves making a promise to God, in what sense is this not a vow, in the light of what has already been said? To which I reply that, between God and us, as between person and person, the nature of promises depends on the intentions of the contracting parties. Each time we make a promise, its content and the way in which we consider ourselves bound by it depend on the intentions of the person making the promise and the way the person to whom the promise is made interprets it. In the case of a temporary commitment, we are talking about a promise not sanctioned by the Church as a public, final vow. The promise which you make to God is personal, the Fraternity receives it and your brothers are witnesses to it, but the promise does not have that public, ecclesial character finally confirmed by the Church. The Fraternity however accepts your promise, since you promise to obey its rule. But it is perfectly understood that the promise made on your own responsibility is accepted by the Prior of the Fraternity as a personal promise to the Fraternity. It is agreed that, if during the period of temporary commitment, you realise that you have not been called to follow this way, you are free to leave. You will then be released from your commitment without the Church's having to intervene. It is enough for the Fraternity to agree, it having for its part made a promise to you.

Temporary commitment therefore constitutes a promise to the Lord who has summoned you, and not merely an act expressing your decision to join the Fraternity and live by its ideals. Your promise is made definitive by perpetual profession. Since you want to give your life definitively to God, you make this promise in preparation for doing so: this is why the promise is concerned with those same evangelical precepts as are perpetual vows. If it were not so, your promise would not be a preparation for perpetual profession, nor a loyal, undeviating response to God.

The Church regards this sort of promise as a private one, in the sense that it binds only you; nonetheless, it is made to God in the Fraternity. One of its immediate consequences is to make you a member of the Fraternity, which means being accepted by its officers and your brothers as a whole, to whom you are now bound and who for their part undertake to help you in every way to carry out what you have promised.

I think I have made this clear. The essence of religious consecration is achieved in the Church when the Church authenticates it. The Church offers your perpetual profession to the Lord as a definitive gift of your life to God. For, as you know, it is quite easy to conceive of living an evangelical community life which is not a consecrated religious one: communities of the former sort the Church calls 'groups of evangelical life'. And nothing prevents you either from putting yourself at the Church's service to carry out a mission and to make a more or less definitive commitment to that. Such is the case, for instance, with societies devoted to spreading the Gospel, as those formerly known under the title *Society of Foreign Missions*. Membership of some of these societies is sanctioned by an oath or promise of obedience to the Superior. These societies make a point of not being religious institutes.

In the past, there was a tendency to confuse distinctions: the fact that these various societies came under the Congregation for Religious and that some of them were distinguished by the wearing of a particular habit, contributed to maintaining the confusion and so to concealing the essential attributes of the consecrated religious life.

Notes

1. The two notes are these:
Note to Mt 8:10 'The faith that Jesus asks for from the outset of his public life, Mk 1:15, and throughout his subsequent career is that disposition of trust and self-abandonment whereby man no longer relies on his own thoughts and resources but commits himself to the power and guiding word of Him in whom he believes, Lk 20:45; Mt 21:25, 32.'
Note to Jn 10:26 'Faith in Jesus implies an inner sympathy with him: one must be "from above", 8:23, "of God", 8:47, "of the truth," 18:37, of his flock, 10:14. Faith presupposes a spiritual affinity with truth, 3:17–21. Cf. Ac 13:48; Rm 8:29f.'
2. Cf. Ac 9:1–18.
3. God said, 'I shall make man in my image, in my own likeness', Gn 1:26.
4. Jesus said, 'You must love the Lord your God with all your heart, with all your soul, and with all your mind. This is the greatest and the first commandment. The second resembles it: You must love your neighbour as yourself. On these two commandments hang the whole Law, and the Prophets too' Mt 22:37–40.
5. Cf. Mt 16:25–26.
6. Cf. Mt 5:48.
7. Mt 6:25–29.
8. Lk 12:16–21.
9. Cf. Lk 2:49.
10. Jn 14:9.
11. 'The Holy Spirit, whom the Father will send in my name, will teach you everything and remind you of all I have said to you', Jn 14:26.
12. Thus, a book has recently been published *Towards a materialistic interpretation of the Gospel of Mark.*
13. Mt 6:24.
14. Jn 12:27.
15. Jn 17:5.
16. 'I came to bring fire to the earth, and how I wish it were blazing already! There is a baptism I must still receive, and how great is my distress till it is over!', Lk 12:49–50. 'Was it not ordained that Christ should suffer and so enter his glory?' Lk 24:26.
17. Cf. Jn 20:17.
18. 'The hour is coming when the dead will leave their graves at the sound of his voice: those who did good will rise again to life, and those who did evil will rise to condemnation', Jn 5:28–29.

19. Is 52:14; 53:3–5.
20. Heb 9:22.
21. Is 1:11–16.
22. Mt 16:21–23; Mk 8:31–33; Lk 9:22.
23. Cf. 1 Co 1:25.
24. Mt 5:48.
25. Address given to the Equipes Notre-Dame, January 16, 1971.
26. Rm 7:15.
27. Cf. Mt 5:21–30.
28. Ga 1:11–12.
29. Ga 1:8.
30. Mt 16:18. The name Cephas means *rock* rather than *stone*. The symbol of the rock was familiar to the Jews, since it occurred frequently in the Old Testament. Yahweh was often called the Rock of Israel. Yahweh was called the Rock on account of his fidelity, Dt 32:4; Is 26:4; 30:29; 44:8; Ps 92:15. The rock from which water gushed in the wilderness was later taken to prefigure Christ, who was also called the corner-stone of the Heavenly Temple.
31. Lk 22:31.
32. Although the word *mediate* is commonly used today, it is not quite accurate in fact, since the Church embodies the mysterious presence of Christ himself.
33. Churchmen's faults, narrowness of mind, unduly rigid dogmatism and political mentality, in a word, their human, intellectual and moral limitations, as well as their frequent ignorance of the facts of contemporary civic and political life, have often been such that non-Christians have played the dominant part in applying the Gospel precepts on a collective scale, as the faithful themselves were incapable of doing this. On this aspect of history, see Jacques Maritain: 'We are not now talking about Christianity as religious Creed and way to eternal life, but as the leaven of the social and political life of peoples and as the bearer of the temporal hope of mankind: not about Christianity as treasure of divine Truth, maintained and propagated by the Church, but about Christianity as historical energy at work in the world. Not in the heights of theology, but in the depths of the secular conscience and secular existence, is where Christianity operates like this, sometimes by taking heretical forms, or even forms of revolt whereby it may seem to be denying its own nature, as though the shattered pieces of the key of Paradise, falling into our sinful existence and combining with the metals of earth, succeeded better in activating the history of this world than does the pure essence of the celestial metal. It was not given to believers integrally faithful to Catholic doctrine, it was given to rationalists in France, to proclaim the rights of man and the rights of the citizen; to Puritans to deal the death-blow to slavery in America; and to atheist communists to abolish the absolutism of the profit-motive in Russia ... The effort to free work and man from the tyranny of money however has its origin in modes of thought in turn derived from the preaching of the Gospel, as did the effort to abolish slavery and that to gain recognition for the rights of the individual. Christ brought a sword into the heart of human history. The human race will not emerge from the era of great sufferings until the hidden stimulating

action, by which the Christian spirit advances and works at horrid cost in the darkness of earthly history, becomes identical with the illuminating action by which the Christian spirit establishes souls in the truth and light of the Kingdom of God' (*Christianity and Democracy*, Editions de la Maison de France, New York, 1943).

34. Lk 24:21.

35. Jn 8:46.

36. 'What right have we then to cast the first stone at the Church, at that poor sinner standing as though accused before her Lord? Do we not fall under the same condemnation as she does, and must we not, like her and with her, appeal to the judgment and mercy of God? . . . How can we seek God in this corporeal existence, receive the Body of the Lord, be baptised into his death, join the procession of the saints and great minds who have loved and remained loyal to the Church, unless we ourselves live in the Church and help to bear the Church's burden, to which we have no doubt ourselves contributed? . . . The physical life of the Church may offer us a weapon against our faith. But it can also make our faith more mature. Were it to sound its death-knell, wouldn't this mean that we had already allowed faith to die in our own hearts?' – K. Rahner, *Is belief possible today?* (*Theoligical Invertigations*, Vol 14, DLT 1976)

37. Ac 9:4.

38. Cf. Mk 4:31.

39. Cf. *Lumen Gentium*, 18.

40. Mk 9:42.

41. Mt 16:18.

42. Cf. 1 Co 2:6f.

43. Cf. Lk 22 32.

44. Cf. 'Whatever the Father does, the Son does too', Jn 5:19. 'My food is to do the will of the One who sent me and to complete his work', 4:34. 'My aim is not to do my own will, but the will of Him who sent me', 5:30. 'He who sent me is with me and has not left me on my own, because I always do what pleases him', 8:29. 'I do exactly what the Father has told me', 14:31.

45. 1 Jn 1:1–3.

46. 'I am astonished at the promptness with which you have turned away from the one who called you and have decided to follow a different version of the Good News. Not that there can be more than one Good News; it is merely that some troublemakers among you want to change the Good News of Christ; and let me warn you that if anyone preaches a version of the Good News different from the one we have already preached to you, whether it be ourselves or an angel from heaven, he is to be condemned. – So now whom am I trying to please – man, or God? Would you say it is men's approval I am looking for? If I still wanted that, I should not be what I am – a servant of Christ,' Ga 1:6–10.

47. Lk 16:29–31.

48. 1 K 19:15 & Jr 1:7f.

49. 1 Co 9:16.

50. Cf. Mt 6:24; Lk 16:9f. We ought to be quite clear what this saying of Christ's means. The men whom we ought to serve are our masters. St Vincent of Paul used to tell his nuns that the poor were to be their masters.

When serving our brothers takes a political form, such service is necessarily geared either to a short- or to a long-term project. The project itself is usually dictated by an ideology. When the latter is based on an anthropocentric philosophy, it offers a very stunted conception of society as the ultimate and supreme evolutionary objective. This objective becomes the absolute yardstick against which the value of all activity is measured. Serving an ideology of this type, a man becomes its prisoner. The master he imposes on himself can only be served to the exclusion of serving any other. Love is the only thing to which man can be enslaved without the destruction of his freedom. As a Shanghai intellectual observed to Alain Peyrefitte in connexion with the Chinese Revolution, 'It does not lay claim to one part of the individual or to one part of the population. It takes over the whole being, the masses in their entirety. It demands unreserved adherence. It is not really possible to be both revolutionary and religious. This would mean: believing in two different religions.' – *When Chine Awakens*, (London, 1976).

51. Mt 14:3–12.
52. Cf. Is 53:1–12.
53. Lk 12:14.
54. Lk 12:16–21.
55. From this point of view, his relationship with Moussa the *amenokal*, head of the tribes of the Hoggar, was exemplary. On the basis of friendship and mutual trust, Father de Foucauld, in advising Moussa, did his best to encourage him to behave more justly and more humanely. But he never did Moussa's job for him. In this respect, he discharged a truly evangelistic mission in the widest sense of the word, since he often appealed to Moussa's faith as a believer.
56. The printing and dissemination of the Bible in every language – the admirable aim of certain missionary societies – stemmed to some degree from this sort of conception about evangelistic responsibility. 'And as you go, proclaim that the Kingdom of God is close at hand . . . If anyone does not make you welcome or listen to what you have to say, when you leave that house or town, shake the dust from your feet', Mt 10:7, 14.
57. 'If a marxist society were to accept political pluralism, freedom of speech and freedom of conscience, it would fall a prey to irreconcilable contradictions. Each type of society creates its own universe, in which everything is consistent' – Alain Peyrefitte, *When China Awakens*.
58. Jn 4:32, 34.59. 'Politics must become our religion, but this can only happen if we have very high ideals, which then transform politics into religion' – Feuerbach.
60. 'Has there ever been such a thing as spontaneous virtue? Is it probable that, when all constraints are abolished and there is no need to worry about being reported to the authorities, people will become naturally good? Has anyone yet discovered a society which truly vindicates Rousseau's theory? It is odd that Marx and Freud should be acclaimed as vindicating instinctual spontaneity. Maoist society is virtuous: but the virtue is collective and imposed by social pressure; while Freud, whom people now try to portray as one of the founders of the permissive society, affords ample proof that there can be no civilisation without repression. 'The majority of men,' he wrote, 'only obey the prohibitions placing limitations on their instinctive desires

where external constraint can make itself felt and when it makes itself feared. They will not refrain from gratifying their cupidity, their aggressiveness and their sexual appetite, they will not hesitate to harm their neighbour by fraud or theft, if this can be done with impunity.' ' – Alain Peyrefitte, *When China Awakens.*

61. Mt 19:21.
62. 1 K 19:9–12.
63. Ex 19:16f.
64. Rule of St. Benedict, Chapter III.
65. 'The evangelical counsels of chastity vowed to God, of poverty and of obedience . . . constitute a divine gift which the Church has received from her Lord and which by his grace she faithfully preserves' – *Lumen Gentium,* 43.
66. *Lumen Gentium,* 44.
67. Jm 1:23.